MEMPHIS

IN THE

JAZZ AGE

D1501005

ROBERT A. LANIER

THE
History
PRESS

Published by The History Press
Charleston, SC

www.historypress.com

First published 2021

Manufactured in the United States

ISBN 9781467148702

Library of Congress Control Number: 2021941046

CONTENTS

PREFACE

This is an ever-so-slightly updated version of my 1979 book, *Memphis in the Twenties*. If you are looking for a plot here, you are making a mistake. This book contains some information about Memphis, Tennessee, in the third decade of the twentieth century. For a number of reasons in which you really would not be interested, I have found the 1920s in America to be fascinating and appealing. I sense in that decade a mixture of sophistication and naïveté that is charming. That the decade was a clear break with the past is attested to by the fact that Frederick Lewis Allen was moved (and able) to write about it objectively only two years after it ended. The clichés about the Roaring Twenties have survived, as have strong images of the personalities who dominated the period, leaving a vivid legend for posterity. Even those who lived through the time will tell you that everyone in America was rich in those days. Of course, they were not. The farmers were chronically in a depressed state economically, and the usual quota of poor were with us. However, a postwar boom, fueled by increased use of consumer credit and speculation, made it seem to many that riches were within fairly easy grasp. In addition, real earnings actually did increase for the average person.

It seems in retrospect that many of the national figures were as vivid and memorable as Dickens characters. The president of the United States for most of the decade, Calvin Coolidge, is one of my special favorites. His personal and political idiosyncrasies have always appealed to me mightily. In popular legend, he appears as a humorless, unsmiling, Scrooge-like figure who uttered banal comments on important matters of the day and slept most of the time. For example, legend has it that Coolidge's only comment on the war debt of the Allied nations to the United States was, "They hired the money, didn't they?" In fact, Coolidge never made such a remark. The transcripts of his press conferences show that he was a loquacious man and an intelligent one. It is true, however, that he extended his Yankee frugality to most aspects of his life. As part of his political philosophy, he is supposed to have said that a president should not worry unduly if he sees three problems looming up ahead. If he will simply wait calmly, said Coolidge, two of the problems will solve themselves and the president will have ample time and energy left with which to handle the one that remains.

The "imperial presidency" of his successors held no appeal for Coolidge. Arthur Schlesinger Jr. would, presumably, have been filled with admiration for President Coolidge's demeanor in that respect. Coolidge singlehandedly restored the prestige of the presidency after it was severely tarnished by revelations of gross theft and graft by President Harding's cronies and paternity by Harding of an illegitimate child while in high office. Saving only Lincoln, perhaps, there has probably never been another president with such an admirably common touch. Coolidge was a kindly man, always keeping a number of dogs about, even in the White House, and he was moved to pay regular visits to the Washington zoo to keep an eye on a small bear that had been given to him as a gift. White House servants regularly observed the small chief executive padding about his private quarters in an old-fashioned nightgown, and he saw no reason why his high office should prevent him from continuing his practice of sitting on the back porch in his rocker after dinner. He wrote his own speeches and occasionally prepared cheese sandwiches for his aides. He apparently took particular delight in teasing his bodyguards and aides by hiding from them or by pressing every buzzer on his desk to summon them all at the same time. Lest it be thought that he was too simple, however, let us recall what he actually said about the war debt:

> *Unless money that is borrowed is repaid, credit cannot be secured in time of necessity....It has been pointed out time and again that this money has to be paid by our taxpayers, unless it is paid by the taxpayers of the countries which borrowed the money. Nations which maintain huge armaments can afford to give consideration to their American obligations. I think that the practical policy to pursue at this time is not to enter into a competitive method of arming ourselves....I should very much prefer that they would take their money and pay us, than on account of any action we took over here, feel that they should take their money and build battleships.*

His philosophy that peacetime government should save money and stay in the background of the national life, giving tax breaks to business (then the employer of most citizens), was endorsed heartily by the people in the 1924 election. If, as has been alleged, Coolidge slept an inordinate amount, it did not disturb the public one bit. Besides, his health was poor. Coolidge was not a stupid man, and the rampant speculation in the stock market affronted his common sense and Calvinist instincts. But he also believed that presidential pronouncements and government tinkering could cause artificial economic disaster. Some believe that Coolidge chose not to run again in 1928 because he sensed a "crash" on the horizon. In any event, the great majority of Americans were content that he should preside over their government while they busied themselves with other matters. They were not looking to the government for a handout, and they certainly did not want the government interfering in their affairs.[1]

Herbert Hoover, who was to succeed Coolidge in 1929, was also later the victim of a number of myths. For example, he never said that Prohibition was a "noble experiment" but that the intention behind it was noble—that is to say, the prevention of alcoholism and its attendant evils. Hoover's worst enemies probably were his jowls and the high starched collars he wore, which were quite out of style by the '20s and made him look like an old fuddy-duddy. Before 1929, however, he was almost universally respected. During World War I and its immediate aftermath, he had been a sort of one-man Marshall Plan, organizing the collection and distribution of food, clothing and medicine to various nationalities that had been ravaged by war and revolution. He was to play the role again in his own country with much success in the Great Flood of 1927. In the period from 1930 to 1933, his methods could not cope with the Great Depression. But from 1921 to 1929, Hoover held the post of secretary of commerce during a decade that saw the expansion not only of conventional "big business" but also new industries of national importance such as radio and aviation. To most Americans of that era, he was the "Great Engineer," and even a usually Democratic state like Tennessee voted to elect him president in 1928. The allegation that he received southern Democratic votes solely because of religious prejudice against Catholic Al Smith, the Democratic candidate for president, is disproved by the stark fact that the state of Mississippi voted for Smith. If Smith could carry Mississippi, then bigotry could not be the deciding factor in the election. Hoover was elected because he was universally respected.

As always, it was not so important how things and people actually were as how they were perceived to be. Someone wrote recently that the youth of the 1920s were the first to see themselves portrayed as a group in mass media such as movies, magazines, newspapers and novels. If they were not already "flaming youth," they soon would be after reading a Scott Fitzgerald novel about themselves, seeing young Joan Crawford dancing the Charleston in a wild movie party or looking at John Held Jr.'s cartoon of their supposed activities. All of that may have little to do with Memphis in the Jazz Age, except that Memphis did share many of the national fads and attitudes and had some strong characters of its own, as you shall see. In this book, I have tried to show a bit of what Memphis was doing during the years from 1924 to 1928, when J. Rowlett Paine was serving his second term as mayor of the city. I chose that period because someone else had already written about Paine's first term and because I think that those were more typically "twenties" years. By then, America had largely shaken its postwar economic and spiritual depression and had not yet reached the fateful, poignant, boom-and-bust year of 1929.

Because so much of the information for this book came from the pages of the *Commercial Appeal*, it is fitting that you should know something about that newspaper and about the remarkable man who was its editor until his death in 1926. (One wonders how future students of local history will fare now that most newspapers are little more than extended handbills.) The *Commercial Appeal*, Memphis's morning newspaper, was born in 1894 as the result of the merger of two of the three remaining Memphis dailies. Its principal owners until well into the '20s included West J. Crawford, William B. Mallory, Luke E. Wright and Lovick P. Miles, all prominent Memphians.

West Crawford was born in Vicksburg, Mississippi, in 1844, served in the Confederate army and became a banker, real estate man and president of the Merchants Cotton Press and Storage Company. He died in 1923. Luke Wright, perhaps the most famous of the group, was a childhood schoolmate of Crawford's and an attorney. He was born in Tennessee in 1846. He was Shelby County district attorney general for eight years, a member of the first U.S. Philippine Commission, governor-general of the newly conquered Philippines, ambassador to Japan and secretary of war under Theodore Roosevelt for a short time. He had also been a bank director and attorney for the Memphis Street Railway Company and other utilities. He died in Memphis in 1922. William Mallory, president of a wholesale grocery company, was a transplanted Virginian who came to Memphis as a Confederate veteran after the Civil War. He was a business partner with Crawford for some time after starting out in the insurance business. He died in 1919. Lovick Miles had been a reporter for the *Commercial Appeal* for five years in the 1890s,

The Commercial Appeal Building, Second Street at Court. *Memphis Heritage.*

including a brief career as Cuban correspondent immediately before the outbreak of the Spanish-American War. He later became a lawyer, joined Wright's law firm and married West Crawford's daughter. After Crawford's death in 1923, he was named to the board of directors of the publishing company, probably because his wife inherited a large amount of its stock. He became president of the publishing company for a brief time in 1926 but probably was never able to devote his full time to the job. He was also prominent in his representation of local utility companies and railroads.[2] There were other stockholders and directors, of course, such as Guston

Fitzhugh, another lawyer who represented utilities.[3] But the founders of 1894—Crawford, Wright and Mallory—were its chief guardians until their deaths. Adherents to the cause of political leader E.H. Crump, who was the subject of bitter criticism by the *Commercial Appeal* throughout the 1920s, alleged that the paper was "the corporation mouthpiece," run by Luke Wright in the interest of his utility clients. This was the view of the *News Scimitar*, an evening rival of the *Commercial Appeal*.[4] When William B. Mallory died in 1919, the *News Scimitar* reported tactfully that he "believed in stating his opinions strongly and forcibly [and]…naturally encountered considerable antagonism."[5]

It was no secret that Mallory took a keen interest in the operation of the paper.[6] When Luke Wright died in 1922, the *Commercial Appeal* was silent about his role in its operation, but the editorial writer went out of his (or her) way to say:

> *For twenty years the present writer, as a member of the staff of this paper, has been in contact with General Wright, and never during that time did* [he] *because of being a stockholder and a director ever suggest anything that might be construed as helpful to any interests he represented as an attorney. On the contrary, he delighted in the independence of the paper.… As a lawyer* [he] *had much to do with the public utility corporations and other large public enterprises.…But never in his whole career did he suggest anything be omitted or anything be written that might favor the cause of any client or any institution that he represented.*[7]

A former reporter pointed out years later that the paper had once criticized a stockholder of the publishing company for not giving generously to the Red Cross during World War I,[8] and during a strike against the Memphis Street Railway Company in 1923, editor C.P.J. Mooney acknowledged the public responsibility of the utility and the public's right to an interest in its affairs. Mooney conceded that such a utility could not adopt the independent attitude that had prevailed thirty years before: "The streetcar company has no right arbitrarily to fix a wage without taking into consideration attending circumstances. The streetcar company has no right to go out of business over night."

He concluded that the wages "probably should be increased."[9] On the other hand, when Crump supporters tried to build a municipal light and gas plant in the same year, Mooney opposed the move as under-financed, riddled with politics and an unwarranted duplication of existing facilities of

C.P.J. Mooney, *Commercial Appeal* editor. *Charlotte Mooney.*

the private company. He asserted that the city was already paying for light plants "established by politicians and sold out at a big profit to the older company." He had no hesitation in suggesting that the price of light and gas could be regulated, expenditures inspected and prices fixed with "a lower profit than the average businessman is willing to accept."[10]

It is true that E.H. Crump was a lifelong, bitter enemy of the local utility companies, and it is undeniable that the owners of the *Commercial Appeal* in that era had close ties with the utilities. However, given the natural antipathy of editor Mooney toward Crump's political methods and the editor's history of attacks on the national "trusts" and plutocrats, it seems unlikely that his editorials were influenced by the owners. They had no need to interfere.[11]

By the 1920s, the *Commercial Appeal* was clearly the most important newspaper in Memphis and the Mid-South. The other two Memphis papers during this time were the *Memphis Press*, owned by the Scripps chain, and the *News Scimitar*, owned since 1921 by young Bernard L. Cohn, a veteran reporter and astute business manager. The *News Scimitar*, claiming a 1922 daily circulation of 60,000 (28,000 in Memphis), was the *Commercial Appeal's* closest rival. The *Commercial Appeal* started an *Evening Appeal* in 1926, but it folded after a few years.[12] The morning *Commercial Appeal*, which called itself "Old Reliable," had the largest daily and the largest Sunday circulation of any paper printed south of the Ohio River or in the Southwest. It had more paid circulation than any paper printed in Richmond, Louisville, Atlanta, Birmingham, New Orleans, Nashville, Dallas, San Antonio, Houston or any other southern city.[13] The circulation was around 100,000 in 1923. This represented approximately a 100 percent increase since 1908, when Mooney became managing editor. The daily circulation was also more than the combined total of its two afternoon competitors. Until the mid-1920s, the paper had its own train to carry its regional editions as far south as Jackson, Mississippi; as far west as Texarkana and Fort Smith, Arkansas; and northward into western Kentucky.[14] During the great Mississippi Valley Flood of 1927, the *Commercial Appeal* proudly maintained service to the stricken areas by dropping the papers to subscribers from airplanes and by broadcasting the news from its radio station, WMC.[15] The newspaper was the training ground for some excellent journalists, such as St. John Waddell and Turner Catledge, later editor of the *New York Times*. The editorial cartoonist J.P. Alley was instrumental in helping the paper win the Pulitzer Prize in 1923 for its battle against the resurgent Ku Klux Klan.[16]

But the man at the helm, the soul of the paper until his death in 1926, was Charles Patrick Joseph Mooney, the editor. Viewed in the context of his time, Mooney emerges as perhaps the most admirable and intelligent of the leading public figures of Memphis in the 1920s. Although having a newspaper at his command can infect a person with an exaggerated self-image and provide him or her with a safe ivory tower from which to hurl thunderbolts at supposed miscreants below, Mooney seems to have genuinely been a man of intellect, integrity and a sense of morality. He was born in Kentucky in 1865, so he was fifty-five years of age when the 1920s began. He graduated from a small Catholic college in Kentucky and taught mathematics for a few years. He studied law and then drifted into working with several southern papers, including the *Evening Scimitar* and the *Commercial Appeal*. He left for New York in 1902, first managing the *New York Daily News* and then joining the Hearst chain. He was an editor of Hearst's *New York American* and then managed the *Chicago Examiner* for three years. While with the Hearst papers, he wrote editorials assailing the Standard Oil trust. When he came back to Memphis, he continued to attack the trusts and the evils of monopoly.[17] In 1908, Mooney returned to his job as managing editor of the *Commercial Appeal*. He was paid a starting salary of $10,000 a year (roughly the equivalent of $180,000 in 2020) and "two or three" shares of stock in the company that owned the paper.[18] Though his title was "managing editor" and not the higher titles "editor" or "editor-in-chief," Mooney was in true control of the paper. (Technically, there was no "editor-in-chief.") He decided not only what news items to run and the editorial policy but also any other question relating to the paper in which he felt sufficient interest to discuss at a directors' meeting.[19]

Mooney was a devout Roman Catholic. He attended mass every morning before work.[20] It is not surprising, therefore, that he did not take kindly to the anti-Catholic antics of the Ku Klux Klan. His religion was fundamentalist in a sense, but as an intelligent man, he could not reject scientific truth. He espoused, therefore, the belief that there could be no conflict between science and religion and that atheism could be defeated with "scientific weapons."[21] He refused to be drawn into a debate on the Virgin Birth and Resurrection, maintaining that some things were beyond comprehension. He urged acceptance of "the entire scheme."[22] He believed that great scientific men of all nations in the past were "profoundly religious," as were the Magna Carta authors. He professed to believe that anarchy was the product of non-religious minds and that communism is the creation of men denying immortality.[23] Mooney also was a patriot. As an Irish American, he was loyal to his native land and to the land of his ancestors. When Ireland gained independence in 1922, the *Commercial Appeal*'s headline (in an editorial) spoke of the "Freedom for which Erin's brave sons have shed their blood through many centuries."[24]

Other headlines tended to be just as colorful (and biased). Crump supporters were referred to as "The Boys," and pro-Crump district attorney general Tyler McLain was referred to as "Fatty" or "the honorable Attorney General." Reference was made to "ballot box obscenities" by the Crump forces.[25] Editorials were usually the product of Mooney and two editorial writers, one of whom was a woman.[26] Young Alfred Mynders, the telegraph editor and son of educator Seymour A. Mynders, was largely responsible, with Mooney, for the lively headlines.[27]

Advancement of the welfare of the African American race had progressed very slowly in the South by the 1920s. As late as 1917, Memphis had witnessed a lynching in which a feeble-minded Black man was chained to a log and burned to death in the presence of a large crowd. The event had been publicly anticipated and reported for days.[28] Most white people of the community regarded whites as inherently superior and Black people as only a step removed from savagery.[29] Remarkably, Mooney rejected this smug concept and maintained, privately at least, that races rise and fall just like nations, depending on factors such as education and environment and not on the shapes or sizes of their skulls.[30] Perhaps it was the Irish in him that rejected the "Anglo-Saxon" claim to superiority. But he was also loyal to his region. In an unpublished editorial, he commented on the situation of the "Negro" in the South and professed to find that "by and large" they had done "mighty well down here." He said that the opportunities were better for them in the South than in the North, if they were decent and God-fearing. He went on:

> *Where in any other place in the United States does the negro* [sic] *get a better break than he does in Memphis?…Here and there negroes have been robbed and they have been exploited. This business is stopping. It does not pay in the long run. The next place, the negro is becoming more intelligent. But more than all, a majority of the whites in any community frown on such a procedure.*[31]

When a potential Ku Klux Klansman wrote to the newspaper to complain that 90 percent of the menial jobs, including ice wagon and truck driver positions, were going to Black workers, Mooney called it "an interesting and difficult situation." He pointed out that in the North, men worked their way up from the bottom, starting with menial labor, while in the South, "white boys are not sought for this sort of work and they do not seek it."[32] Confronted with the Klan's racial and religious bigotry, Mooney's instinct for order and justice was aroused:

> *At this time, when all good Americans should be engaged in fostering and maintaining sectional, racial and religious goodwill and friendship, there should be no place for persons or organizations inspired by a contrary purpose. Real respect for law should bring liberality of thought and*

tolerance of purpose. Agitators of sectional, racial or religious hatreds are committing the greatest sort of offense against the spirit and aims of the United States.[33]

That is not to say, of course, that Mooney was opposed to the segregation of the races, then in full force throughout the South. When President Warren Harding spoke to a Black group in Alabama about their welfare, Mooney's regional pride was wounded:

There is no race problem in the South. Nobody is talking about the social equality of the races. A sensible negro does not want social equality with the white man and sane white men know that such a thing is impossible. The best thought in the South wants the negro to be protected in life, liberty and property. He must have the right to a job. He should be permitted to keep what he honestly earns. His outbreaks are a crime against the law and a problem of lawfulness and not a problem of race, and the problem of lawfulness is nationwide. The negroes around Memphis are getting along mighty well.... We shall continue to get along mighty well if people stop lecturing us on [the] race problem.[34]

Mooney scanned the poverty of the surrounding region and noted the slavish dependence on the whims of the cotton market because of a one-crop economy. Early in his career as editor, he became a crusader for diversification of crops.[35]

His attitude toward the prohibition of liquor was that he hated liquor but was opposed to the deceit and hypocrisy of Prohibition laws where public sentiment was against them and enforcement was unlikely.[36] By 1923, he had decided that, on the whole, Prohibition was a good thing because he thought there were fewer drunkards than there had been ten years before.[37]

It was in the arena of politics, however, that Mooney was at his most effective. Whether ridiculing the renascent Klan or indignantly exposing the machinations of E.H. Crump and his supporters, the editor fought like a tiger for his sense of law and morality. Crump made his first race for mayor in 1909, only one year after Mooney had returned to Memphis permanently. At first, the *Commercial Appeal* was neutral toward Crump. It soon became clear, however, that Crump was grabbing for power, and his methods aroused Mooney's ire. The editor always made a point of the fact that he did not accuse Crump of personal dishonesty, nor did he usually oppose Crump's governmental policies. He even opposed the state ouster law,

Senator K.D. McKellar. *Hooks Memphis Public Library.*

passed by Crump's enemies for the purpose of removing him from office. What he could not tolerate, however, were gross political shenanigans such as voting frauds, an attempt to hold the offices of mayor and sheriff simultaneously, passing public offices around like volleyballs and protecting saloons and other illegal businesses. Occasionally, Mooney and Crump found themselves unexpectedly on the same side in a particular election. Generally, however, the warfare continued until Mooney's pen was stilled by death.

In 1923, Mooney's control of the paper was further recognized by his appointment as president of the publishing company. In 1927, less than a year after his death, the paper was bought by Nashvillians Luke Lea and Rogers Caldwell to serve their own ends. Thereafter, the paper's war with Crump fizzled out and was no more. It is a tribute to Mooney that "Old Reliable" was never the same after his death.[38] However, thanks to its yellowed, almost century-old pages (now on microfilm), we can relive a little bit of Memphis history, bearing in mind our present-day experiences with the shortcomings of newspapers as accurate reporters of what really happens in the world.

Another important source of information for this little study was the papers of Senator Kenneth D. McKellar. McKellar served as United States senator from Tennessee from 1917 until the voters finally replaced him with Albert Gore Sr. in 1953. Born in Alabama, he had started out as a young lawyer in Memphis and served in the U.S. House of Representatives until his election to the Senate. He was a lifelong close ally, but not a flunky, of E.H. Crump. He was a bachelor and devoted most of his waking hours to his duties as senator. He was a staunch Democrat and, for his time and the state he represented, something of a liberal. He was philosophically right at home when the New Deal came into office. On rare occasions, he and Crump were on opposite sides of the political fence. However, his opposition to monopolies and big utilities usually placed him squarely in Crump's camp. His loyalty to the Democratic Party did not prevent him from maintaining cordial relations with Tennessee Republicans. The following letter to my grandfather, found among the McKellar papers, was interesting to me:

Honorable J.G. Crumbliss   *November 4, 1924*
Knoxville, Tennessee
Dear Senator:

    While of course, I was against you politically in the campaign, yet I take the greatest pleasure in congratulating you, and in saying that I believe the interests of your district will be well represented in the Legislature.

    I wish for you a most pleasant and agreeable service at Nashville, and am confident you will reflect great credit upon yourself and upon the city that you represent.

    With kindest regards, I am,

                 Sincerely yours,
                 Kenneth D. McKellar

Apparently, my Republican grandfather had supported McKellar in the 1922 senatorial race, and McKellar had written to express his gratitude at that time. My grandfather replied in a whimsical vein, with unwitting irony:

Honorable Kenneth D. McKellar   *December 6, 1922*
United States Senator
Washington, D.C.
My Dear Senator:

    I thank you for your very kind favor of November 25. It does seem that the people in Tennessee had most thoroughly made up their minds that they did not want a change in United States Senators at this period, and I am now of the opinion that in about "24 more years" you will occasionally hear it remarked— "old Senator McKellar ought to have one more term before retiring."

    Congratulations and many good wishes for your health and happiness.

                 Yours truly,
                 J.G. Crumbliss

In fact, that is precisely what did happen twenty-four years later, in 1946, when McKellar was reelected to his last term in office, having served as president *pro tempore* of the senate and next in line for the presidency from 1945 to 1949, when Truman became president. McKellar sought another term in 1952, but the voters had had enough, and he only had a short time to live.

Rummaging through the McKellar papers, which were almost totally disorganized except chronologically, was a fascinating experience. Not only did the names of many individuals of both national and local fame and infamy appear, but the wide variety of requests that a senator must answer was made clear. There were telegrams asking for intervention with the immigration service to permit the entry to the United States of someone's foreign relative, perched expectantly in Mexico, Canada or Cuba. One such request was tersely refused by the government because the applicant was "suffering from a loathsome disease." Another thing that sticks in the mind is the number of requests from constituents for free seed, which the senator would dutifully forward to the Department of Agriculture for certain gratification. The increase in volume and variety of requests brought about by the lapse of almost a century must be truly awesome. One wonders whether the seed supply has been exhausted.

Well, as the announcer on the old *Lone Ranger* radio and television shows used to say, "return with us now to those thrilling days of yesteryear." If you are from Memphis, you may derive some pleasure from comparing the city then and now. If you are not a Memphian and by some miracle decide to read this book, I can only hope that you will get some satisfaction from comparing your city during that time with Memphis. In any event, thank you for reading this far.

An apology is no doubt due to the reader at this point. When this little book was written in 1978, many sources readily available today, especially from the internet, were not in existence or were beyond the author's reach. This is especially true of the scholarship about African American life and history. But it is hoped that the kind reader can accept this *mea culpa* and overlook "what might have been" and accept this effort for whatever it is worth. The author has lived long enough to see the rules and fashions regarding the capitalization of references to the races, and the words used to describe them, change many times. What was once considered courteous and respectful (such as "colored" for Black people) became unacceptable. Terms once considered neutral and technical were ultimately rejected. The publishers of this book have decided that the racial description "Black" shall be spelled with the first letter capitalized, while reference to "white" persons shall not. As the old saying goes, "I don't have a dog in that fight." I don't wish to offend anyone and have chosen to use the racial descriptions that seem to be currently acceptable to African Americans.

Finally, to steal from Mark Twain, persons attempting to find a motive in this narrative will be prosecuted, persons attempting to find a moral in it will be banished, and persons attempting to find a plot in it will be shot.

—Robert A. Lanier
August 4, 2020

When at the first I took my pen in hand thus for to write; I did not understand that I at all should make a little book in such a mode; nay, I had undertook to make another, which when almost done, before I was aware, I this begun.

—*John Bunyan,* The Pilgrim's Progress

CHAPTER 1

MEMPHIS IN A NEW ERA

America was ready for the 1920s. It has been noted that sometime between 1915 and 1920, the United States became an "urban nation," when, for the first time in its history, more people lived in the cities than in rural areas.[39] The significance of this bare statistical fact was accentuated by the First World War, which attracted thousands to the war industries of the cities, mobilized and unified the nation as never before and ended what Henry May has called "American Innocence."[40] There was more truth than poetry in the wartime song that asked how America could keep its millions of ex-soldiers and sailors down on the farm after they had seen "Paree." More important, how could they return to their prewar provincialism?

Most significant of all, perhaps, was the rise of what George Mowry has called "the urban mind" in the period after 1919.[41] With the impetus given by the Great War, the sense of national unity and identity was intensified by technological advances such as the inexpensive, mass-produced automobile and the mass media, such as motion pictures, radio and modern newspapers. Automobiles enabled rural Americans to maintain contact with, and feel a part of, nearby urban areas. Motion pictures, radio and newspapers rapidly expanded the size of their audiences, binding rural areas to their neighboring cities and the cities to one another, eroding or eradicating many provincial attitudes and developing a new national consciousness by mass production of goods and nationwide advertising of them.[42]

Cities, whether located in the North or the South, began to exhibit more similarities than differences. Chief among the similarities was a reverence for business and commercial expansion. A short depression had followed the end of the world war, bringing cancellation of fat government contracts and beginning the lowering of agricultural prices that so strongly affected the rural South. Cotton was faced with the renewed competition of European and Japanese mills.[43] The depression in industry, however, was essentially over by 1923, and most of the country was ready for a new era of prosperity.[44] In cities all across the nation, the term "progressive" no longer had its prewar connotation of social reform and industrial restraint. "Progress" had come to mean, through some subtle process, the encouragement and expansion of business as a goal in itself.[45] The southern cities bowed to no one in their adherence to the new principles of progress. If anything, they were even more impelled by the prospect of realizing the revitalized, industrial "New South," which had occupied the minds of many southerners since the 1880s.[46]

Memphis, Tennessee, had ceased to be a "river town" and become a city at the turn of the century, when its population was pushed over the 100,000 level by sweeping annexations. The city became a unique part of the progressive era in the early years of the century when, influenced by vigorous leaders like Edward Hull Crump, it reformed itself politically, if not socially.[47] By the end of the First World War and the brief depression of 1920–23, Memphis was very much a part of the new urban nation, feeling and reacting to the dominant trends of the period that affected all of the larger American cities, although its viewpoint was still colored to a considerable extent by nostalgia for its regional past.

CHAPTER 2

THE GROWING CITY

To those who think along such lines, the small earthquake that jolted Memphis on New Year's Eve 1923 might have served as a herald of the nation's recovery from the postwar depression and its entrance into an era of booming prosperity.[48] And into this era the South and Memphis threw themselves, as W.J. Cash put it, "with the most complete abandon."[49] Memphis, like other cities, towns and hamlets of the South, had become passionate in its quest for progress and the urge to surpass its rivals.[50] Part of this rivalry in urban areas was in population growth. Although most southern states continued to be predominantly rural during this period, the situation was undergoing great change: 52 percent of the population in Florida was now urban, as was 40 percent of Louisiana and 32 percent of Tennessee.[51]

When, in 1924, the Federal Census Bureau estimated the population of Memphis at only 172,000, Mayor (and former businessman) J. Rowlett Paine was indignant. It was as though a slur had been cast upon the city's reputation. The bureau had estimated Memphis's population by multiplying the city's annual increase in population during the period from 1910 to 1920 by the number of years since 1920. Mayor Paine, somewhat apoplectic, called this method "ridiculous" and claimed that the size of school enrollments and the number of houses erected were better indicators. The city's homicide and death rate—a sensitive statistic for Memphians at the time—looked much worse in the context of a smaller population. Mayor Paine claimed a population of over 200,000, and the new city directory did

Madison Avenue looking west toward the post office and river. *Hooks Memphis Public Library.*

list 193,250 names. The *Commercial Appeal*, Memphis's leading newspaper, felt safe in predicting a population of 300,000 by 1934. (As events would have it, this figure was not attained by that time.) Undaunted, the Census Bureau estimated Memphis to have 178,900 souls in 1927 and would not withdraw its figure.[52]

Despite these minor setbacks, Memphis was moving into a new era and seemed to know it. "Memphis is still booming," wrote young lawyer and future mayor Watkins Overton to Senator McKellar in 1924.[53] Looking back on the just completed year of 1925, the *Commercial Appeal* noted:

Riding on the crest of a wave of prosperity, side by side with many other cities throughout the nation, Memphis has just passed through the best year from a business standpoint it has ever experienced. Not even in the flush, inflated years of 1919 and 1920, when cotton sold at 30 to 40 cents a pound did the amount of money that changed hands through the Memphis banks equal the volume handled through 1925.[54]

Bank clearings in that year were $1,239,000,000, or $49 million more than in 1920, the previous record.[55] In view of such prosperity, and encouraged nationally by sloganeers like Arthur Brisbane and Emile Coué, there is little wonder that Memphis adopted the prevailing optimism. The *Commercial Appeal* on January 3, 1926, commented:

Memphis in the beginning of 1926 has fine hotels. It has a magnificent auditorium. It has developing schools. It has churches in process of construction. The capacity of its oldest charity hospital is being doubled....It has more golf grounds....It has an improved murder record. It has good judges and little politics. The public utilities are efficient. The telephone service is good. The gas and electric lighting plants have been put into modern working order. They are out for business and their management is decently polite. The streetcar company limps a little needing more cars but the other two companies carry it along....So, all things considered, the people of Memphis have reason to feel that we have made big strides in '25 and we should view 1926 with a serene confidence in the growth and prosperity of our beloved city.[56]

Who could question this "serene confidence" in prosperity when the president of the New York Stock Exchange stated that depressions were a thing of the past[57] and Calvin Coolidge, the president of the United States, specifically expressed his confidence in a stock market based on unprecedented prices and credit speculation?[58] Secretary of Commerce Herbert Hoover could. Although anticipating increased prosperity, Hoover cautioned against reckless optimism and lack of financial control.[59] But such warnings did not dampen southern spirits.

"Over the whole land hung the incessant machine-gun rattle of riveting hammers; in many places the streets were like those of a rebuilding war area, with the yawning walls of old buildings coming down and of new buildings going up."[60]

Memphis, too, was caught up in the passion for rebuilding. In 1924, seven major commercial structures were in the process of construction in Memphis. A new building for Lowenstein's department store was erected at Main and Monroe on the site of the historic old Hotel Peabody. The Security Building, later the Union Planters national bank, was going up at Union and Front. The Columbian Mutual Tower, the city's "skyscraper" (and a smaller copy of New York's Woolworth Building), went up on Main, just north of Court Square, and the new Cotton Exchange Building grew on what had been Cotton Row (now Front Street) at Union. Two new hotels, the Claridge on North Main Street and the Adler on South Main Street, opened their doors at opposite ends of downtown.[61] The famous Peabody Hotel, moving from its historic site at Main and Monroe, opened the doors of its new sumptuous, $5 million structure on September 1, 1925, for some 1,200 guests at the initial banquet and ball. The hotel business was good. Less than a month later, most Memphis hotels, including the Peabody, were filled to capacity.[62] The auditorium portion of the long-sought Ellis Auditorium and Market House opened on October 18, 1924, with John Philip Sousa and his band playing to the 14,000 first-nighters. Ten thousand people were turned away. The first regularly scheduled performers in the new building were the San Carlo Opera Company, which opened on October 20 with a week of performances including *Pagliacci*, *Madama Butterfly*, *Il Trovatore*, *Aida* and a different ballet each night.[63]

In 1924, one in every seven Americans had an automobile, and they seemed to have more Fords than any other kind.[64] Citizens of the Memphis area had bought fifty-eight thousand Fords in 1923, and the demand was such that the local assembly plant, with its meager crew of 300, was often not up to its task. It was, therefore, decided in January 1924 to erect a new assembly plant near Riverside Park on Riverside Boulevard at South Parkway West, which was on the south side of town near the Mississippi River. The $1.2 million structure was to be one of seventeen Ford assembly plants erected in 1924 and employed nearly 1,200 people.[65]

The Gothic structures of Southwestern College added grace and dignity to the building boom in Memphis in 1924. The college had at last been lured from its former home in Clarksville, Tennessee, by the donation of a one-hundred-acre campus and some $800,000.[66] Charles E. Diehl,

Columbian Mutual Tower under construction, 1924. *Lincoln American Life Insurance Co.*

president of the Presbyterian school, explained that Clarksville was chosen over Memphis in 1874 because at the time Memphis, with its recurrent yellow fever epidemics, was considered unhealthy and Clarksville was considered more cooperative. The new college building program started on a small scale. It was decided to begin with a few lasting buildings rather

Above: Lobby of the newly opened Peabody Hotel, 1925. *Hooks Memphis Public Library.*

Opposite, top: Ladies lunching at the Peabody Hotel Tea Room off the lobby, 1926. *Author's collection.*

Opposite, bottom: The audience at the Auditorium opening with John Philip Sousa's band. *Hooks Memphis Public Library.*

than many second-rate ones. President Diehl said that they were able to build with stone more cheaply than with brick because they had their own quarry in Arkansas.[67] The location of Southwestern College at Memphis contributed in another way to the physical growth of the city. The greatest residential development in any single section of the city from 1923 to 1925 was in the area around the college site. Throughout Memphis, this was a period of remarkable growth in residential building. All previous records in residence construction were surpassed in 1924 for, in that year, housing for 11,500 more people was provided. There were, in fact, practically no development sites left untouched within the city limits by 1926.[68]

Without question, Memphis was experiencing one of its periods of significant physical change. Even a new county jail and criminal courts building was erected, opening for business in 1925, a little over a year after forty-one prisoners had dug their way out of the old jail at Front and Auction.[69] In February 1924, Memphis issued building permits on work costing $1,189,980 (perhaps $15 million in 2020)[70] and led the other southern states in building for that month.[71] Mayor Paine toured the principal building sites and felt obliged to warn the contractors that if they did not stop blocking streets and alleys and start covering all the sidewalks so that people would not have to walk in the street, he would have the police make arrests.[72]

There were other indices of Memphis's growth and prosperity. Memphis had long been a rail center, and in 1923, the largest number of railroad cars on record were loaded with revenue freight.[73] Fast new passenger trains running from Memphis were inaugurated. The Rock Island Line's first daily Memphis-Californian to Los Angeles pulled out the afternoon of December 30, 1923, and Mayor Paine was on hand to congratulate the Illinois Central Railroad as the *Chickasaw* departed for St. Louis on January 13, 1924.[74] Memphis hoped to make equal progress with the air age, which seemed to be dawning, and anticipated having a full-fledged airport as early as 1925. A visiting army engineer suggested that Mud Island would be a good location for such a facility.[75] However, by 1927, the year of Charles Lindbergh's transatlantic flight, the best that Memphis could boast was tiny Armstrong Field at Woodstock, Tennessee, south of Millington, near the Illinois Central Railroad track. This provided no obstacle to globe-trotting Italian air force Colonel Francesco de Pinedo, who parked his seaplane on the river behind the post office and was greeted by Mayor Paine and a large delegation in May 1927.[76]

Memphis progressed with the nation in communications as well. Dial telephone service was inaugurated in May 1925, and radio station WMC, owned by the *Commercial Appeal*, went on the air in January 1923, only a little more than two years after the first broadcasting station in the country.[77] By this time, the country was becoming aware of radio and was purchasing radio sets in ever-increasing numbers. By the end of the decade, a radio in the home was virtually as commonplace as a television is now. Thousands in the Mid-South listened to WMC's broadcasts from "Memphis, Way Down in Dixie," as they billed themselves.

With the growth of the city had come problems. There were more people than ever, and a growing number of them were equipped with one of the mass-produced automobiles. Farmers and urbanites motored on the city's

Paine inaugurates a new passenger train, presumably with the Manitou's blessing. *Hooks Memphis Public Library.*

streets in unprecedented numbers and with a disregard for safety that Memphis detractors say still exists. In 1922, Memphis had the third-highest automobile death rate in the country: 24.4 per 100,000 population. Police commissioner Thomas Allen blamed the problem on the fact that, although state law set the speed limit at twenty miles per hour, the city had not even been limiting drivers to thirty miles per hour very strictly. Moved by the statistics, Commissioner Allen, along with his traffic police, met with the new city judge, Clifford Davis, in January 1924. A decision was reached to arrest anyone driving over twenty-five miles per hour.[78] In the face of the new police policy, Memphians slowed down temporarily.[79] Fatality statistics continued to mount, however. The streets were particularly unhealthy for pedestrians, who constituted most of the 94 traffic fatalities in 1925.[80] In another attempt to cope with the city's growing traffic problem, Union Avenue became, in January 1924, the first official arterial highway in Memphis. This meant that all east- and westbound traffic would have absolute right of way over intersecting streets on the six-lane (two for parking) avenue.[81] One traffic victory that Memphis would eventually win was not in sight in 1924. It was said of downtown Memphis in June of that year, "At every corner, there's

Thomas H. Allen. *Hooks Memphis Public Library.*

a noise riot in progress, a clanging, yelling, screaming, whistling, honking commotion." It seemed to be the custom for drivers to try to "toot their way through traffic." Commissioner Allen hopefully sent out word to police to arrest motorists with any unusually obnoxious propensity to sound their horns and sirens.[82]

And so the city grew and seemed to prosper. What of the average Memphian? His food was not always relatively cheap by today's standards. Ham was forty-five cents (equal to perhaps five dollars in 2020) a pound, coffee thirty-six cents (four dollars) a pound, eggs twenty-seven cents (three dollars) a dozen, butter forty-two cents (five dollars) for four sticks and a can of Campbell's soup eight cents (perhaps a dollar and fifty cents in 2020 money).[83] On the other hand, federal income taxes were lighter in those days on the average citizen. In fiscal year 1922, the federal government still collected its greatest revenue from customs duties.[84] The normal income tax on a married man with no dependents was as follows:

Net Income	Tax
$2,000	$0.00
$3,000	$7.50
$4,000	$22.50
$5,000	$37.50
$6,000	$52.50
$7,000	$75.00
$8,000	$150.00

In 1926, this tax was drastically reduced.[85]

Little wonder if a Memphian's hand reached pensively for his checkbook when he read the full-page advertisement in the *Commercial Appeal* inviting him to "share in the millions of dollars of profits" and "lay the foundation for [his] fortune" in Florida real estate for only $100 down.[86] How could he know that the Florida "bubble" was soon to burst?

In the South, as in the rest of the nation, the period of business expansion brought a new veneration for business. Good business helped prosperity, and prosperity was good for the country. Business and the "boosting" thereof

Sears executive Julius Rosenwald (*with glasses*) hears Mayor Paine dedicate the new Sears Roebuck building, 1927. *Hooks Memphis Public Library.*

was a new passion. The president of the United States professed to believe that the business of America *was* business,[87] and Governor Harry Byrd of Virginia stated that "the administration of government should be efficiently conducted along the lines of well-organized business enterprises."[88] The words *progress* and *progressive* largely came to mean to the southerner, as to most Americans of the period, business efficiency and development, rather than social and political reform.[89] Large northern corporations maintained regional branch offices in Memphis, creating a new business entity for the South in the local agent of the corporation. He was a businessman of prestige in the community but also a new kind of "overseer" in the "new urban plantation" of the absentee northern owners.[90]

Other aspects of the new progressivism locally became apparent in 1924, when the dairy businessmen of the Memphis area, led by Dabney H. Crump, cousin of political leader E.H. Crump, organized to end milk price cutting and discuss dividing the city into spheres of influence.[91] Community spirit could sometimes take on ominous overtones, as seen in a telegram in April

Madison Avenue looking west from Fourth Street. *Hooks Memphis Public Library.*

1924 from cotton man J.H. Riechman to Tennessee's U.S. senator McKellar. The local Community Fund drive had just closed with a $20,000 deficit, perhaps because the Loew's and Pantages theater interests had ignored a "request" that a liberal contribution be made. Riechman, a political associate of E.H. Crump, reminded McKellar of the help "all of our friends in the legislature" had given on behalf of allowing Sunday theatrical and motion picture performances and lowering admission taxes. "They are making [a] serious mistake in their attitude," concluded Riechman, meaningfully.[92]

So, there sat the city on the bluffs, growing and sharing, at least superficially, in the national rhythms of prosperity and "progress." To the *Commercial Appeal*, government was the only hovering threat to prosperity:

> *American people are rapidly becoming slaves of their taxes. The burden of government is now about four per cent. of all the wealth of the country....*
> *More than 2,000,000 of the 7,000,000 who paid* [federal income] *taxes last year will not have to pay taxes this year....In 1925* [the expense of the federal government] *had gone up to eleven and one*

half billion dollars....In a few years the government will begin to subsidize the farmers, which is the beginning of a slow progress of suicide on the part of the Republic. Yet everything looks fine....Stocks are high, money is cheap. Trains are filled with people going to and from California. Florida is filled with spenders, buyers, and sellers. Billion dollar trusts are being formed.... We are going at a great rate. The country is on wheels. The highways are becoming so crowded that a lot are taking to the air and the end of it all is not in sight, but is like a cancer. The cancer...is in the state.[93]

CHAPTER 3

STRONG IN MIND AND BODY

For all its emphasis on business growth and prosperity, Memphis had not entirely forgotten the progressive spirit of the early days of the century. When E.H. Crump became mayor of Memphis in 1909, his administration placed much emphasis on expanding public services. The newly organized commission government of that year placed the general supervision of public health under the mayor's office, and the City Hospital, a charitable institution supported by the city, was thoroughly renovated. In 1911, the University of Tennessee located part of its medical school at Memphis, and it operated in conjunction with the City Hospital.[94] In 1920, after consolidating all of the university's medical school branches in Memphis, the relationship between the City Hospital (then known as the General Hospital) and the medical school was strengthened by an agreement whereby the city would maintain the hospital and allow the medical students to use it for training. In return, the university agreed to nominate and oversee the hospital's staff of doctors.[95]

As 1924 opened, Memphis had reason to be proud of its medical facilities. The Memphis General Hospital, owned and supported by the city for treatment of persons too poor to pay for medical care, was rated as a class "A" institution by the American College of Surgeons. The university erected the pathology laboratory located on the hospital grounds, and the members of the winter staff of the hospital were nominated by the university and elected by the board of trustees. Bonds issued in 1921 built the isolation wing, and another issue in 1923 provided funds for a maternity wing and remodeled kitchen. The hospital managed a budget surplus for 1923. No patients were turned away from the General Hospital for lack of funds. Most of the patients were African Americans, and well over 85 percent of the patients treated in the wards were charity cases. In 1923, 7,559 patients were received, of whom 1,763 were accident cases. It seemed to be a matter of pride that "the staff never draws the color line" toward patients.[96]

The city public health department could also boast that it had both white and Black nurses, ready day and night to answer calls to homes anywhere in the city. Their services were free to the poor.[97] As a result of the efforts of Governor Austin Peay and Shelby County legislators such as Marion Boyd and Watkins Overton, the college of medicine of the state university received half a million dollars for growth in 1924 and 1925.[98]

Few hospitals in the United States admitted as many patients in 1923 as Memphis's Baptist Hospital, which cared for 10,943 persons. Supporting Mayor Paine's denial of the accusation that Memphis was the "murder capital," the Baptist Hospital released this breakdown on the residence of those 324 persons who died within its walls in 1923:

Memphis: 124
Mississippi: 67
Arkansas: 59
Tennessee (outside the city): 62
Missouri: 8
Kentucky: 2
Louisiana: 1
South Carolina: 1[99]

St. Joseph's Hospital admitted 5,735 patients in 1923, of whom 2,862 were charity cases.[100] The Oakville Sanitarium for tuberculosis, which was opened near Memphis in July 1921, seemed to be making progress. Of its 715 patients, 80 had their conditions arrested and 154 showed sufficient improvement to be discharged. The regimen consisted largely of lots of fresh air and rest. More than twenty-five years were to pass before antibiotics would make tuberculosis a rare disease in Memphis. Of the sanitarium's 374 patients in 1923, 216 were white and 158 were listed as "colored," a polite term in those days for African Americans.[101]

As might be expected, Memphis schools were experiencing a period of growth and expansion. In 1924, there were some 31,000 children enrolled in Memphis public schools. Of these, 19,000 were whites and 12,000 were

African Americans. Three new Black schools had been built in 1923, and two were being constructed in 1924. Five additional white schools had been erected within virtually the same period, and bids were let in early 1924 for the one-hundred-classroom North Memphis High School on Manassas, now named for L.C. Humes, president of the board of education at that time. Bids were also taken for a new Black industrial school and for additions to existing schools. In all, $500,000 ($7,500,000 today) worth of schools were contracted for in 1924. The school system had long operated with a deficit, but by 1924, bond issues, city taxes and state school grants had put the board of education back on its feet financially. Of course, all of this was long before the federal government contributed anything to local education or was expected to.[102]

In the area of higher education, Memphis was lacking. As previously mentioned, Southwestern at Memphis (now Rhodes College), a small, Presbyterian liberal arts college, was in the process of locating to Memphis during this period and reopened in 1925. High standards were to be maintained, but the results were yet to come.[103] In 1912, the state had opened a small teachers' college, referred to in those days as a "normal school," on the eastern outskirts of the city near Buntyn. Originally called the West Tennessee State Normal School (now the University of Memphis), it had grown somewhat by the 1920s. Its grade school used as a training laboratory for the student teachers (and thus called the "Normal Training School") erected a separate building on campus in 1923, which operated under the auspices of the city board of education. However, the college remained primarily a training ground for schoolteachers.[104] Investigating the source of the word "normal" when used in connection with a teachers' school is an enterprise not worth pursuing here.

Christian Brothers College, founded in 1870 by a Roman Catholic brotherhood, still operated on a small scale in a dilapidated antebellum building on Adams Street, near the downtown area, and could not yet offer a bachelor's degree.[105] Memphis had a law school, calling itself the University of Memphis, but it was a proprietary business, operating only at night with limited facilities, and was not accredited.[106] This did not, of course, prevent it from turning out numerous practitioners at the bar. Even in those days, there never seems to have been a shortage of lawyers.

If facilities for the higher education of whites were limited, the facilities for African Americans were nearly nonexistent. The idea of Black students attending the white colleges was quite unthinkable and illegal under the state segregation law. Howe Institute, with 350 Black students, was owned

Southwestern (now Rhodes) College, newly built in 1924. *Hooks Memphis Public Library.*

and controlled by African Americans, with financial assistance from whites. LeMoyne Institute, supported by tuition fees and northern benevolence, had 436 students in 1924. Neither school could offer a degree, and neither was accredited.[107]

Thirty years would have to pass before Memphis could offer a respectable semblance of advanced education to prospective students of either race. On the other hand, the city's medical facilities, aided by state funds and concern by local officials for the public's physical well-being, were a source of pride during the 1920s and have remained so.

CHAPTER 4

THE MID-SOUTH

The visitor to Memphis during this era, sitting in his room in, say, the Claridge Hotel on Main Street, looking at the construction work going on virtually outside his window and reading editorials in the *Commercial Appeal* about the city's prosperity, might assume that the whole tri-state area was similarly blessed. It was true enough that a brand-new town was growing up across the river. West Memphis, Arkansas, was formally incorporated in June 1927, with a population of seven hundred.[108] But in his copy of the newspaper, the visitor might find, upon close inspection, the Crown Medicine Company's advertisement for a surefire pellagra cure, a hint that all might not share in the prosperity of Memphis.[109] And if he troubled to cross the Harahan bridge to Arkansas and explore the area around newly incorporated West Memphis, he would find the standard home for a tenant in that part of the country to be a wooden box containing one room sixteen by sixteen feet and a lean-to in the rear sixteen by eight feet. Some of the structures were inferior to the stables built for the livestock, and the *Commercial Appeal* blamed the migration of farm laborers to the North partly on such inadequate housing.[110]

There seems no question that the surrounding area was poor. It was depressed. A retired Meridian capitalist blamed Mississippi's poverty on the legislature's failure for twenty years to offer incentives for industry to locate in the state.[111] W.J. Cash notes that even when northern industry was lured south in this period by free sites and tax waivers on a large scale, little was done to enrich the area. Profits flowed back to the North, and much of the South became merely an exploited colony.[112] It seems clear that the depression of Memphis's rural neighbors was caused by their dependence almost solely on cotton. Less cotton was being worn as clothing,[113] and foreign competition in growing and milling was increasing.[114] Too much cotton was being grown. The cotton crop of 1925 was the second-largest crop in history up to that time.[115] In the fall of 1926, the decline of cotton prices below the cost of production caused Governor Henry L. Whitfield of Mississippi to call for a convention of the governors of fourteen cotton-growing states. At the convention in Memphis, a campaign was launched to reduce acreage and to form cotton-holding pools. The latter met with some success. Credit organizations were arranged to assist those who wished to hold their cotton off the ten-cent market. There was proposed a voluntary pool, to be financed by bankers and merchants, to take four million bales off the market and hold it for two years if necessary. The market reacted to this proposal by rising only one-half a cent. The convention paid the customary lip service to diversification of crops, but it was virtually admitted that no hope existed for voluntary acreage control. The past had taught that whatever was gained by withholding acreage one year was lost the next, in the scramble for volume.[116]

It is not surprising, therefore, that cotton buyers, even in the form of Russian Communists such as Alexis Gumberg, vice president of the All-Russia Textile Syndicate, were welcomed without too many qualms about their political backgrounds. (The Soviet Union was not then recognized as the legal government of Russia by the United States.)[117] Memphis was an island of relative prosperity in a stagnant rural economic sea.

CHAPTER 5

POLITICS

Since 1909, Memphis had been governed by a mayor and board of commissioners, each separately elected directly by the people and each having generally equal power. This "commission" form of government was new to American municipal government at that time, and Memphis was one of the first cities to have it. Edward Hull Crump, along with other influential Memphians, had been a prime mover in introducing the commission government, which was considered a vast improvement over the previous mayor and legislative council system. The latter had fragmented the city into districts, encouraging ward-heeling and decreasing the independence and efficiency of governmental operation.[118] On the other hand, commission government helped to ensure that minorities could not elect a commissioner. The commission form of government came to suit Crump's form of power politics admirably.

In 1910, after leading the successful battle for a legislative change in the form of city government, E.H. Crump became mayor. Crump, a transplanted Mississippian, had successfully challenged an entrenched city "machine" and even obtained a change in the form of city government. It soon became clear, however, that his thirst for power was great, and he set about building his own machine. The most outlandish political gymnastics took place, including Crump's attempt in 1914 to be both mayor and sheriff simultaneously, passing the mayorship on to two other men in the course of one morning in 1916, illegally "voting" illiterate African Americans, paying city budget deficits with bond issues, protecting political allies who abused

E.H. Crump and his lieutenant, Frank "Roxy" Rice. *Hooks Memphis Public Library.*

their offices, ignoring prohibition laws and using government employees to perform political tasks. Despite the enemies he made with his ruthless acts of political retaliation against those who opposed him, he seems never to have been accused of personal dishonesty. Some noted, however, that his insurance agency did not exactly suffer from his position of power. Crump was forty-six in 1920, thinking about retirement from active politics but actually near his prime. His six-year tenure of office as mayor had been marked by vigorous attacks on problems of public health, education and recreation. His squabbles with privately owned power and transportation companies culminated in his ouster from office in 1916, after suit was filed against him for failure to enforce the state's prohibition on the sale of alcohol. Although Crump opposed prohibition and refused strenuously to enforce it against saloonkeepers (who had been his valuable political allies), it seems likely that the ouster was inspired by his enemies among the public utility interests.[119] The period following Crump's removal was one of political confusion, with Crump continuing as the dominant force in the county, if not the city.[120]

In 1919, J. Rowlett Paine, a wholesale grocer, had been elected mayor on an independent, "good government" ticket. Paine was something of a *rara avis* in this era of colorful adopted Memphians. He was a native of Memphis and a product of the Memphis school system. He had spent most of his adult life, like Clarence Saunders, in the grocery business, although without Saunders's spectacular success and showmanship. However, by dint of steady, sound work, he held high executive office with the A.B. Treadwell Company when he was drafted for mayor in 1919. He was forty-one when he took office in 1920. His running mates for the commission were also elected and tended to follow Paine's lead. Most notable among the other commissioners was the able Major Thomas H. Allen, a World War I veteran, who became commissioner of Fire and Police.[121] Paine ran an honest and independent administration.[122] The *Commercial Appeal*, which had supported him, was moved to comment in 1924 that Paine's administration was peculiarly free of politics.[123] Paine had gained some prestige by calmly and successfully resisting a firemen's strike shortly after he took office, in which all the firemen resigned.[124]

For E.H. Crump, former mayor and "boss" of Shelby County, the period of Paine's two terms as mayor was one of consolidation. It was a time to continue placing his friends in key political jobs and to secure his own financial well-being by building up his insurance and brokerage firm.[125] Crump held the lucrative office of county trustee from 1916 until 1924, and during this period, his machine was strengthened by the addition of loyal followers to the county payroll.[126] When he relinquished the office of county trustee in September 1924, the *Commercial Appeal* evaluated his position:

> He leaves his office with his political prestige unimpaired. In fact, it is doubtful whether his personal influence ever reached so widely and deeply as it does on his retirement from office. His allies control practically all the branches of the county government. A sheriff of his own choice continues his duties for a term of two years. An amiable County Court was sworn in yesterday for six years. After four years of aloofness and indifference he has concluded an understanding with the city administration and between them they will control the next legislative delegation, if the regular slate is elected in November.
>
> The last outpost that might have been considered doubtful has apparently hoisted a friendly flag. Governor Austin Peay has appointed Tyler McLain Attorney General to succeed Sam Bates.[127]

Crump's secretary boasted that his employer "took a commanding part in electing U.S. senators, governors, congressmen, judges and city and county officials of every kind" and that he had spent days "virtually directing both branches of the state legislature at Nashville." No one seriously believed that Crump's retirement as trustee meant his retirement from politics.[128]

Apart from the patronage derived from long years in public office, the "secret" of Crump's political power, both before and after 1924, was detailed organization. It is said that he maintained an up-to-date card index of all Memphis voters. His lieutenants were stationed in the offices of government and in banks, civic clubs, cultural associations, favored labor unions and churches.[129] Boycotts and police harassment were not unknown for those who failed to contribute to campaign coffers.[130]

One factor that made Crump's task of organization easier was the state poll tax. By 1924, only 20 percent of the adult population of Tennessee took part in elections. The tax of over two dollars for most males (perhaps thirty dollars in today's money) apparently discouraged many potential voters from registering and gave the man who could get poll taxes paid inordinate power. Crump's forces took full advantage of the situation, busily rounding up friendly voters and seeing that their poll taxes were paid. The ability to deliver overwhelming majorities in Shelby County was to give Crump and Shelby County disproportionate power in state politics as well.[131] The *Commercial Appeal*, however, saw nothing sinister in the poll tax and considered it a bargain and a boon to the school fund, which benefited from it.[132]

As 1924 opened, therefore, E.H. Crump exercised control of the county government that, if not absolute, was based on a form of "majority rule." But Crump did not control the city mayor or commissioners of the Paine administration.[133] Crump had neither supported nor opposed Paine in his first race for mayor in 1919 but had a definite falling out with him in 1921. First, Paine failed to reappoint a Crump supporter to the Park Commission.[134] Then the mayor opposed a Crump-supported private act in the legislature that would have allowed the city to build a gas and light plant. As a result of Paine's opposition, GOP governor Alf Taylor vetoed the bill. In Crump's view, this and other behavior by Paine smacked of cooperation with the hated power interests. Paine seemed to be following the advice of people whose views differed from Crump's, and the mayor was entirely too independent of the county leader for their relations to be entirely harmonious.[135]

Nevertheless, in the city election of 1923, at the last minute, Crump had thrown the support of his organization behind Paine's ticket in order to defeat the strong and threatening Ku Klux Klan ticket. The Klan, quiescent since Reconstruction, was reborn in 1915 and revitalized by a shrewd publicity agent so that, by this time, it was a potent force nationally. The organization housed not only white supremacists but also millions of average Americans, frustrated variously by the imagined threats of communism, Roman Catholicism, Zionism, the "foreign element" and the changing times in general. The Klan's national leaders had not yet been discredited for venality and immorality in 1923, and the movement was at its peak.[136] The Memphis city election of 1923 marked the Klan's formal entrance into local politics. The local Klan was less ideological than political.[137] When the votes were counted, Paine's ticket for the city commission was elected, although Klan candidate (and estranged former secretary to Paine) Clifford Davis was elected city judge. There was little doubt in the minds of Crump supporters that an accurate count would have given the entire election to the Klan.[138]

CHAPTER 6

INAUGURATION

On January 1, 1924, the reelected city commission was sworn in at the city commission chambers at the county courthouse. Present were Mayor Paine; commissioner of public utilities Horace Johnson; fire and police commissioner Thomas H. Allen; Charles R. Shannon, commissioner of accounts and finance; and Henry N. Howe, commissioner of streets, bridges and sewers. The mayor made a brief address in which he declared that the attention of the administration during the previous four years had been devoted principally to the material aspects of the city's progress: streets, viaducts, sewers and other physical improvements. With this program well underway, he said, he and his colleagues proposed to devote their energies to the social life of the city and the human interests of the people. He hinted at the need for intellectual and social progress, and the *Commercial Appeal* warned that "the tribe of Babbitts would get little comfort from the Mayor's second inaugural."[139]

Across the street in the city court building, a more colorful ceremony took place. Ku Klux Klan leaders—including Coroner N.T. Ingram and Joe Wood, defeated candidate for mayor—gathered with city commissioners and many other interested citizens to witness the fruits of the only Klan victory: the inauguration of Clifford Davis as city judge. Pappalardo's Orchestra entertained the packed courtroom with a "programme of music" until, at 11:10 a.m., it burst forth with "Dixie" as Commissioner Allen led Davis and outgoing judge L.T. Fitzhugh through a line of police to the bench. Circuit court judge Pittman swore in Davis and urged his friends to expect no favors

Inauguration of Mayor Paine and the city commission. *Hooks Memphis Public Library.*

but to let him do his job. Davis said that he felt that politics was over with and that he only wanted to do a good job.[140]

Davis did not escape criticism as a result of his association with the Klan, however tenuous it may have been. When, a few months later, he fined two Klansmen only one dollar each for fighting, the *Commercial Appeal* chided him for not recusing himself and commented on his election:

> *Davis was elected city judge by a flattering majority. Nightly for weeks preceding the election, cyclops and kleagles, kluckers and cliquers, hung upon his eloquent words, and cheered him on to victory. Being an upright man, he attracted to his candidacy several thousand voters free from racial and religious prejudices, and these, added to followers of wizards and goblins, made the calling and election sure. The others on the ticket were left in the murk to mourn with the whangdoodles.[141]*

The Klan had not been eliminated as a political factor in Shelby County by the election of 1923. In January 1924, as time for the convening of the

City commissioners (*left to right*) Horace Johnson, John B. Edgar, Mayor Paine, Charles Shannon and Thomas H. Allen. *Hooks Memphis Public Library*.

county court (the county legislative body) grew near, reports of Klan activity spread. Klansmen had been working day and night in an attempt to control the votes of the court members, or "squires," as they were called, from the rural districts of the county. Squire Houston of Fisherville was the Klan candidate for chairman of the county court, and Klansmen spread the word that those who voted against Houston would be swept from office by Klan votes in the upcoming summer election.

E.H. Crump, leader of the dominant political element in the county, supported Squire Gowen of Bartlett for chairman and stated that his victory by a vote of 20–7 was a foregone conclusion.[142] Crump, however, did not feel sufficiently strong politically to precipitate both the chairman's election and the rumored removal of the coroner, N.T. Ingram, at the same time.[143] Ingram was a past candidate for "Exalted Cyclops" of the Klan and, according to the *Commercial Appeal*, was "regarded as the Nestor of the Kluckers in the city and county."[144] His Klan activities, coupled with the fact that the coroner would succeed to the office in case of its vacancy, made Ingram a prime target in Crump's fight against the Klan.[145] As expected,

Gowen was elected on January 7. Sheriff Oliver Perry died on the same day.[146] The problem of Coroner Ingram now had to be met.

Under the law, the county court could elect a new sheriff after three days' notice on the first day of the term of court. After three days' notice, on January 14, the Crump-dominated county court overwhelmingly elected W.S. Knight, a Crump stalwart and one of its members, to be sheriff until the August general election. Knight made bond, took his oath and was then and there served with a chancery court temporary injunction forbidding him to act as sheriff. N.T. Ingram had brought suit, alleging that the county court could not elect a sheriff at that term, since the "first day" had passed. Knight's attorneys, including County Attorney W.T. McLain, McLain's young law partner Lois D. Bejach and Phil M. Canale, answered that the obvious intent of the statute was only to govern vacancies occurring during the recess of the court.[147] The friendly lawsuit temporarily ended when the chancellor decided that he was without jurisdiction in the matter but hinted that he favored Knight's contentions.[148]

Crump's next problem was to remove Ingram as coroner, and a way was soon found. A pro-Crump squire rose in the county court chamber and offered a resolution declaring the office of coroner vacant. The reason? It had been discovered that Coroner Ingram's election of October 1922 was not on the court's minutes.[149] When the resolution was read, Ingram rose to his feet. "I'm the coroner," he shouted. "I was elected in October 1922, and every member of this court knows it. I was elected by acclamation. Look at my bond. That will show that I was elected." Wild disorder followed. There were cries of "Throw him out!" "Let him talk!" "It's an outrage!" and "He's got it coming!" Squire Connell of Eads said that, although he was not himself a Klansman, he felt bound to defend Ingram because the coroner was a Confederate veteran. Ingram freely interrupted the debate from time to time. When finally given the floor again by chairman Gowen, he stated that it was not his fault that the minutes did not record his election. "Ask the clerk about it. He knows," Ingram concluded, helplessly.

The clerk, Ed Crenshaw, was contrite. "It was my fault," he said. "The memorandum was misplaced." County attorney (and Crumpite) W.T. McLain gave the court the benefit of his opinion that the absence of reference to Ingram's election in the minutes voided the election. The court thereupon voted 20–7 to declare the coroner's office vacant and to elect a successor. The court also proceeded to attach additional precincts to the strongly pro-Klan Twenty-Fifth Ward.[150]

Ingram once again sought relief in chancery court, but with little more success. Chancellor Israel Peres denied that his court had jurisdiction but indicated that if it did, it might supply the omission on the county court books.[151] By the ouster of Ingram, the Klan had suffered a serious political defeat that did nothing to prevent the looming split in its Shelby County ranks.[152] Word leaked out in February that, following a recent visit by Imperial Wizard Hiram Evans, the charter of the Shelby Klan was revoked and it was no longer affiliated with the original Atlanta Klan. Soon, street brawls broke out between rival groups of Klansmen.[153] It was a preview of the dissension that would soon wrack the Klan all over the country.[154]

CHAPTER 7

CRUMP, THE POLITICAL LEADER

In early 1924, E.H. Crump let it be known among his friends that he would seek one "last" public office. He wanted to be elected delegate-at-large to the Democratic National Convention. Since that required election by the state Democratic convention in Nashville, it was not a foregone conclusion. Crump was confident,[155] however, and those who saw him at this time thought that they had never seen him in better form.[156] For some reason, Crump seems to have really wanted the insignificant job of delegate and took particular delight in his prospects of election.[157] Well he might, for despite his apparent lack of opposition, his friends went to work on his behalf immediately. Crump's friend U.S. senator Kenneth McKellar busied himself, making sure that the "boys will see to it that no hitch comes in the proceeding."[158] Friends constantly assured Crump of his victory.[159] When the convention met in Nashville in May, Crump got his wish. The Shelby County delegation, 353 strong filling fifteen Pullman cars, pulled into Nashville and marched the streets with banners marked, "McKellar and Crump," and "Crump and McKellar." Governor Peay made no opposition to Crump's election, and the Shelby leader got the unanimous vote of every county in the state. Crump was delighted.[160] Even Mayor Paine, only recently allied somewhat tenuously with the Crump forces, was seen at the convention wearing a "Shelby for Crump" badge.[161]

Crump was soon on his way to the Democratic National Convention in New York City, at the Madison Square Garden.[162] As a delegate, Crump voted for the planks favoring the entrance of the United States to the League

Left to right: Walter Chandler, Mayor Paine, presidential candidate William Gibbs McAdoo and others, 1924. *Hooks Memphis Public Library*.

of Nations and was among those delegates taking a stand condemning the Ku Klux Klan.[163] As June ended and July opened, it became apparent that William Gibbs McAdoo, Crump's preference, and the favorite of the majority of delegates in the early balloting, would not get sufficient votes for the nomination. After 103 exhausting ballots, John Davis, a compromise candidate, was selected.[164] Crump returned to Memphis, tired but with his smile intact. He advised reporters, "Don't ask me anything about the convention. I understand that McAdoo and Smith had a fight for several hundreds of ballots and John W. Davis finally won. That is all I will risk."[165]

No sooner had Crump returned than he plunged into a new battle against old political enemies and the still present threat of the Ku Klux Klan.

Crump had hardly announced his intention in late May 1924 to quit active politics for business when new political rumors began to fly. Encouraged, perhaps, by Crump's imminent retirement from public office, Klansmen let it be known that they were planning a concerted attempt to elect sympathizers in the elections to be held in August 1924. The August voting would include a Democratic primary election, which would virtually decide who was to be the next United States senator, governor of the state and representatives to the General Assembly (the legislature) in Nashville. (Only rarely was a Republican elected governor of Tennessee at that time.) There would at the same time be held a county election to fill the offices of sheriff, trustee and county court squires. The Klan seemed most intent on the county offices.[166]

In late June, county court squire Will Taylor announced his candidacy for sheriff, intimating that he expected countywide support from Klansmen, although he disavowed any "disposition to encourage racial or religious prejudices." The city and county administrations conferred and selected Frank Hoyt Gailor, a Rhodes scholar, assistant city attorney and son of an Episcopal bishop, as their candidate to succeed Crump as now-salaried county trustee. Former mayor and veteran campaigner J.J. Williams also announced for the post. It was said that he was counting largely on being backed by the Ku Klux Klan.[167] To meet the Klan threat, the city and county organizations began working in early July on a joint slate of candidates, especially for representatives to the legislature.[168] The meetings produced a legislative ticket heavy with lawyers but featuring a newspaperman and a businessman. The delegation contained both Crump and Paine supporters.[169] Neither side claimed any tactical advantage in the selections, and the two factions seemed to be working in close harmony.[170]

As the race for trustee formed, Crump returned to one of his favorite campaign weapons: the newspaper advertisement. Radio was in its infancy, and television was still on the drawing boards. In an advertisement on July 30 titled "J.J. Williams Is Trying to Hog It All," Crump teased Williams, a turn-of-the-century mayor, for continually running for public office. "It matters not what the election is for," Crump wrote, "or how often they come in the city and county; he just must run." He went on to list the offices sought by Williams since 1880 and revived the charge that Williams had fraudulently sought to conceal his ineligibility (due to the residence requirement) for the mayor's office in the 1919 race. Finally, he charged that Williams was a Klansman until 1923 and was "playing with them again."[171]

Mayor Paine campaigned with Sheriff Knight and Frank Gailor, accompanying them on handshaking tours about the city. The candidates were confident of victory if all their supporters could be gotten to the polls. According to the *Commercial Appeal*, the city organization's strongholds consisted of the densely populated part of the city bounded on the west by Dunlap, on the north by North Parkway, on the east by Cooper and on the south by Central. Taylor and Williams were hoping for a tremendous vote in the seven wards, including the blue-collar Fairgrounds and Binghampton areas, which had been heavily pro-Klan in the 1923 city election.[172]

The *Commercial Appeal* endorsed the city administration's choices and observed that "we should like to see men in the county offices and in the legislature who would catch step with the city administration and cooperate in further efforts for a progressive Memphis and Shelby County."[173]

The *News Scimitar*, the leading evening newspaper, had long been friendly to Crump, and Crump expected its support in the county race. The publication was edited during this period by Bernard Lake Cohn, a scholarly Memphian (by way of New York) who set the paper's policy on local politics. The *News Scimitar*'s past alliance with Crump seems to have been attributable partly to its rivalry with the morning *Commercial Appeal*, which usually opposed Crump,[174] and partly to the revenue derived from legal advertising placed by Crump and his officeholding supporters.[175] In 1924, however, the *News Scimitar* demanded Crump's support of incumbent U.S. senator John K. Shields in his race against Lawrence D. Tyson of Knoxville, in return for support of the Crump-based county ticket. When Crump refused, the paper would not actively support his candidates and began to refer to the county organization in its columns as "ballot box wizards" and "the machine."[176] In the 1926 elections, the *News Scimitar* returned to the Crump fold, but shortly thereafter, the paper was purchased by the Scripps-Howard chain, which already owned the anti-Crump evening *Memphis Press*. Upon the arrival of Edward J. Meeman from Knoxville in 1931 to edit the newly formed *Press Scimitar*, the paper's opposition to Crump became permanent.[177]

As election day in the all-important Democratic primary drew near, Mayor Paine felt constrained by "considerable street talk" to warn that he and the city commission would allow no election irregularities. The "street talk" doubtless stemmed in part from the indignation expressed by Klansmen over what they considered the theft of their victory in the 1923 city election.[178] On election day, August 7, 1924, very little disorder was reported outside of a few arrests in the county. Although city police and sheriff's deputies had been put on twenty-four-hour duty, there were only nine arrests. The *News Scimitar*, which had grumbled that Crump's election commissioner, John Brown, had allowed "conditions favorable to fraud," noted that the election was a "tame affair" with the expected "machine victory." It expressed the general surprise, however, at the weakness of the Ku Klux Klan vote.[179]

When the ballots were counted, Frank Gailor, Sheriff Knight and Dave Wells were elected by wide margins. Wells was the allies' candidate for county tax assessor. Squire Will Taylor received 10,248 presumably pro-

Klan votes to Knight's 16,286.[180] Taylor scored heavily in the rural areas, carrying twenty of the thirty-seven rural districts of the county and tying in one. Of the city's seventy-four precincts, Taylor and Williams carried only sixteen, less than one-fourth of the total. Williams was the weaker of the candidates, Gailor having defeated him by an almost two-to-one ratio. In three city precincts that split their votes between the two tickets, Taylor was the winning candidate. Of the sixteen city precincts that voted for Taylor and Williams, ten were from neighborhoods inhabited predominantly by poor whites, a nearly three-to-one majority being given by the second and third precincts of the Thirteenth Ward, which was composed largely of railroad workers. The other six precincts consisted mainly of middle-class white voters.

In the 1923 city election, the first in which the local Ku Klux Klan made a serious effort to gain elective office, the Klan secured heavy majorities in the Thirteenth, Twenty-Fourth, Twenty-Eighth, Twenty-Ninth and Thirty-Third Wards of the city. The Twenty-Fourth Ward had a three-to-one Black majority and predictably overwhelmed the Klan in the 1924 race, although the vote was light. The Twenty-Ninth "Fairgrounds" Ward and the Thirty-Third Ward in the Binghampton area were conceded to the Klan unofficially even before the election. These areas, consisting mostly of lower middle-class white railroad workers and laborers at the Binghampton Motor Works, were a hotbed of Klan sentiment and repeated their heavy support of Klan candidates. The Twenty-Fifth Ward, with a majority of lower-income whites, turned its vote heavily against the Klan in 1924, but the Twenty-Eighth and Twenty-Ninth Wards, mostly middle-class whites, stayed solidly with the Klan. The KKK also captured, for the first time, the Eighteenth Ward, composed of middle- and upper-class whites.[181] The seven wards in which African Americans constituted a majority went solidly for the candidates backed by Paine and Crump, and the balance of the white-dominated city wards followed suit with varying degrees of enthusiasm.[182]

Although it had not managed to elect an official to office in 1924, the Klan retained its voting strength virtually undiminished by its defeat in 1923. The Klan's percentage of the total vote in the August 1924 elections stood at 38 percent as opposed to 39 percent in the white-hot campaign of 1923. The Klan organization was still a powerful force to be reckoned with in Shelby County if it could remain united and use its power judiciously. As subsequent events were to prove, it was unable to do either.[183]

For Crump and Paine, of course, the most significant fact was that victory had been achieved. When the results were announced, E.H. Crump led a brass band and hundreds of cheering followers through the downtown streets. Mayor Paine joined the procession for a while. The parade "stormed" the police station on Adams and then threaded its way to the Commercial Appeal building, opposite Court Square, for a serenade. This became a traditional gesture of Crump's to tease *Commercial Appeal* editor C.P.J. Mooney. Although they had found themselves on the same side in the August election, Mooney must have realized that Crump's serenade that night was a boast of power as well as a salute to an ally.[184] Mayor Paine might well have pondered how much of the victory was due to Crump's efficient political organization and how little was attributable to his own efforts.

Much talk was heard around Memphis in August 1924 to the effect that the net result of the county election was to eliminate the Ku Klux Klan as an issue in local politics.[185] E.H. Crump was not ready to disregard the Klan as a political factor yet. When a rumor persisted that a split between the city and county forces was imminent, due to Crump's supposed dissatisfaction with the Democratic legislative ticket, Crump publicly announced:

> *There is absolutely no discord and there will not be any.…*[The] *ticket will be elected in November, notwithstanding that there is a movement on foot for a coalition ticket of the Ku Klux Klan and some Republicans. The city and county organizations are united and ready for them and invite their opposition. Troublemakers and those disappointed at the defeat of Senator Shields may as well know this right now.*[186]

Squire Will Taylor, the defeated candidate for sheriff, brought suit in September to declare the election void, charging the Knight forces with voting irregularities. He alleged that Knight men had taken all the election official jobs and that four hundred armed deputies named by Knight had intimidated voters. He further charged that many of the voter registrations were fraudulent and many ballots miscounted.[187] When the case was subsequently tried, a courtroom filled with Klansmen and county leaders, including Crump, watched the proceedings.[188] Taylor won a hollow victory in the first round when the court held the election void but allowed Knight to hold office until a new election.[189] Ten days of hearings had been held on alleged fraud, but county forces disproved a sufficient number of the charges to convince many that the result of the election was not changed by any misconduct.[190] The final victory was Crump's. He jubilantly wrote to Senator McKellar in August 1925, "Today our crowd is much elated over the sweeping victory of Knight over Taylor in the Supreme Court, which throws the entire litigation out for good."[191] Despite continuing rumors of some sort of alliance between the Klan and elements of the GOP, Crump was publicly confident of victory in the November general election.[192] On a visit to Nashville to meet with state Democratic headquarters, he predicted "a fine majority" for the ticket.[193] All factions of the Shelby County Democratic Party were united, and the *Commercial Appeal* urged public contributions to the campaign fund.[194]

The November election was an unexciting anti-climax. The Democratic candidates carried the county handily.[195]

CHAPTER 8

JAZZ AGE MEMPHIANS

For Memphis, as for most of the rest of urban America, this was the decade that has become known as the Roaring Twenties, the Jazz Age and the Era of Flaming Youth. The world war's end marked the beginning of a revolt against the idealism and puritanism of the recent American past.[196] If Memphians were shocked in 1925 to read that 433 Vassar College girls admitted that they smoked, they were probably just as stunned by the behavior of their offspring at home.[197] Jazz music and wild new dances bid fair in the minds of many to destroy the younger generation. A Kansas doctor, commenting on the recent death of a teenage girl while dancing, warned that dancing the Charleston could be fatal. The vigorous movements of the dance could cause inflammation of the peritoneum, the doctor advised.[198] The music (or something) seemed to be already eroding the sanctity of marriage. Marion, Arkansas, had become a "quickie" marriage center for impatient Memphis youth.[199] Canute-like, the *Commercial Appeal* spoke out against the tide of events:

> *Marriage and jazz—when marriages are performed there ought to be some regard for the solemnity of the act….The other day in Memphis a young man got married to the step of the Charleston, a new and dirty dance, which is one of the latest offerings of musical degenerates to art. The ceremony was performed by a squire.*
>
> *The other night, for the first time in 3 or 4 years, we went to a picture show. The leader of the orchestra played the Meditation from "Thais."*

Then after he played it he "jazzed" it. That leader, instead of bowing his thanks to the audience, ought to have bowed his head in shame that beautiful music is butchered and debauched and then offered to the public in the shape of a dish of jazz.[200]

As though to provide more evidence of youth's irrevocable deviation from the path of righteousness, some two hundred students of Humes High School actually went on strike at the sound of a fire bell at 10:00 a.m. on September 15, 1925. Scores of Memphis versions of the comic strip character Harold Teen filed happily out of their morning classes and piled into their automobiles. Later, a mass protest rally was held on campus with a Black jazz band to lend a festive air to the proceedings. Before the speeches began, a number of demonstrations of the Charleston delighted the assembled patrons of higher learning. The reason for the strike? The city school superintendent would not add eleventh and twelfth grades to the school. "This will not do," sputtered the *Commercial Appeal*. "This is a revolt against authority."[201] Perhaps the editorial writer would not have worried so much about Memphis's youth if he had known that the following January, Central High School would graduate a future newspaper columnist of renown, Walter Stewart, and a noted historian of Memphis, Gerald Capers.[202] As always, the older generation was feigning shock at the new.

Considering its population and regional importance in the 1920s, Memphis appears to have been lacking in its support of the more serious forms of cultural activity. Memphis was not without some of the fine arts, however. From 1919 to 1924, the Memphis Municipal Symphony Orchestra, sponsored partly by the music committee of the chamber of commerce, had operated without a deficit. In 1924, however, it had poor public response in its drive to raise $4,000 ($50,000 today) to avoid disbanding. Concerts were given at schools and such cultural locales as the Goodwyn Institute at Third and Madison.[203]

It took a group of public-spirited local businessmen to guarantee Memphis some exposure to grand opera. In 1924, they hired the San Carlo Grand Opera Company for a full season.[204] In 1925, the Memphis Civic Music League was able to sponsor a week of grand opera, attracting such stars as Mary Garden and Feodor Chaliapin, along with the Chicago Civic Opera and its ballet.[205]

In 1924, Rosa Lee of the famous riverboat line family offered her home on Adams to the Memphis Art Academy for its headquarters.[206] The academy, though still struggling, was one of the oldest in the South.[207] From time to time, famous musical artists such as Sergei Rachmaninoff and Irish tenor John McCormack gave stopover performances in the Bluff City.[208] By and large, however, the city seems to have offered considerable justification for H.L. Mencken's jibe that the South was "the Sahara of the Bozart."[209]

The average evening for middle-class white Memphians seems to have consisted of dancing rather than opera and the movies rather than concerts. Memphians could dance at Dreamland Gardens on Linden at Bellevue, across from Central High School, or at the Shrine Building Roof, where twenty-five cents admitted one to the ballroom, which was enlivened by the music of Bob Miller's Orchestra and the dancing of Elma Chighizola. On "white only" nights, whites could see such famous Black jazz and blues stars as Bessie Smith at the Palace on Beale Street.[210] Memphis jug band music, played for pennies on the street by Black musicians, became so popular that in 1927, it was included in the first phonograph recording made in Tennessee.

The Gene Lewis–Olga Worth stock company of actors settled in Memphis and for several years provided "live" drama and melodrama at the Lyric Theater. They were joined by the Lysle (later Lyle) Talbot Players in 1928 at the Lyceum Theater.[211] For the most part, however, Memphians were entertained by vaudeville acts and motion pictures, the two invariably running concurrently at the same theaters. The favorite theaters were the Orpheum on Main at Beale (reopened in 1928); the Lyric on Madison; and the Majestic, Lyceum, Pantages (later the Warner) and Loew's State, all on Main. The movies until 1928 were all silent, of course, except for piano, organ or orchestral accompaniment. Before or after cowboy Tom Mix, exotic Rudolph Valentino or glamorous

An ad for Gene Lewis–Olga Worth stock company. *Vincent Astor.*

The Lyceum Theater, when showing movies. *Vincent Astor.*

Gloria Swanson finished their performances on the screen, live acts such as Alexander, "the world's master psychologist," appeared on stage.[212] Unexpected entertainment was provided in 1923 when the old Orpheum (formerly the Grand Opera House) burned down during a performance. When the new Orpheum was completed in 1928, it represented one of the best examples of the gilded age of motion picture palaces, which was then in full swing across the country. Inspired by the Roxy in New York, the country was dotted with fantastic movie palaces with ornamentation outdoing in garishness the finest opera houses in the world, if lapses of taste and excesses were overlooked. Ben M. Hall, in his excellent book *The Best Remaining Seats*, reminds of the importance of movie-going in those days:

> *For Mama, another world lay beyond the solid bronze box office where the marcelled blonde sat (beside the rose in the bud vase) and zipped out the tickets, sent the change rattling down the chute, read* Photoplay, *and buffed her nails—all without interrupting her telephone conversation. Heaven only knew what exotic promise waited behind the velvet ropes in the lobby, what ecstasy was to be tasted in the perfumed half-darkness of the loges.*[213]

The entrance corridor of Loew's State movie theater on Main Street. *Vincent Astor.*

There were those who mourned the popularity of the less serious forms of entertainment. When movie star Mabel Normand was discovered to have been involved with a murdered motion picture director in Hollywood, the Memphis city censor board banned her pictures permanently, warning that to allow her films to continue to be shown "would serve notice to our youth that you can commit any folly you please and get away with it." The *Commercial Appeal* applauded this move and urged the censor board to ban any picture "which for any reason is detrimental, in their opinion, to the moral welfare of the people....It is not absolutely necessary that the picture itself be indecent."[214] Of equal concern to the newspaper was the belief that movies and vaudeville had driven out legitimate theater so that it was difficult to book high-class traveling shows for lack of proper housing and staging facilities.[215]

In retrospect, it appears that Memphis, influenced by the growing popularity of motion pictures and radio, was drifting into that long period of cultural sterility that lasted well into the 1950s and perhaps has not entirely passed. Opera, concerts, ballet, serious drama and other vestiges of a slower and more aristocratic era hung on as the half-concealed hobby of the rich and the few. For most middle- and lower-class Memphians, by the mid-1920s, the "movies" and radio (which was rapidly becoming widespread) were enough.

CHAPTER 9

MEMPHIS, THE MURDER CAPITAL

I n 1923, Dr. Frederick L. Hoffman, statistician for the Prudential Life Insurance Company, startled Memphians by stating that their homicide rate of 67.4 per 100,000 population made them the "murder capital of America."[216] Mayor Rowlett Paine was particularly sensitive about the matter and charged that Dr. Hoffman's comparative tables were misleading, since cities like Atlanta and Birmingham, cities "with a large proportion of Negroes," were not listed in the tables.[217] Paine even telegraphed United States senator Kenneth McKellar in an attempt to get U.S. secretary of commerce Herbert Hoover to "adjust" the Commerce Department statistics to show the proportion of nonresident deaths.[218] In 1925, Paine refused even to release to Hoffman the city's records on homicides. In retaliation, Hoffman wrote an article for an insurance journal attacking Paine's attempt to conceal "the facts of the situation that the city unquestionably has the highest murder rate on record." Hoffman considered immaterial the defense raised by Memphians that large numbers of wounded non-Memphians sought medical care in Memphis and expired there for that reason alone. Hoffman professed to believe that the "lawless element…finds in Memphis the kind of environment it is seeking for the furtherance of its criminal pursuits."[219] Famous rustic comic Will Rogers, in Memphis for a show at Ellis Auditorium, teased Mayor Paine, saying, "What kind of a city is this, if you have to shoot a man to get him to come here?"[220]

Hoffman was not without some statistical justification for the label that he put on the city. In 1922, with a population of roughly 160,000, Memphis had 79 homicides. The figure reportedly dropped by only 1 death in 1923.[221] In early 1924, killings were coming at the rate of 1 every four days.[222]

Taking stock of the 1923 homicides (and using the terminology of the day), the city police reported the following statistics:

CLASS OF VICTIMS

Homicides	78
White males	11
White females	4
Colored males	49
Colored females	14

SEX

White males killed by white males	9
White males killed by white females	1
White males killed by colored males	1
White males killed by unknown	1
White females killed by white males	4
Colored males killed by colored males	26
Colored males killed by colored females	14
Colored males killed by white males	6
Colored females killed by colored males	11
Colored females killed by colored females	2
Colored males killed by unknown parties	3

CAUSE OF DEATH

Clubbed	1
Rifle shot	1
Ice pick	2
Shotgun	5
Knife	18
Pistol	51[223]

The last execution for a Memphis killing had been in 1919.[224] Mayor Paine proposed to solve whatever problem Memphis had by setting up a crime commission to correct law enforcement procedures, which he felt gave the criminal too many breaks. He also felt that more attention could be given to closing up "various notorious dives."[225] Would this have solved the problem? There seems to have been more than a little merit to the argument that the Memphis medical center was the repository, albeit involuntarily, of an unusually large number of dying residents of the tri-state area who had come to Memphis for a patch-up.[226] There was also the possibility that the city's own outlook did not retard violence as well as might have been expected. We find the *Commercial Appeal* as late as the summer of 1924 calling for a sharp decrease in the practice of carrying a pistol.[227] The all-too-frequent practice by the police of shooting misdemeanor suspects attempting to escape led the same newspaper to comment that "all our people are tolerant of murder.... Men kill one another down here for little or nothing. Killing seems to be all in a day's work.... The shooting habit seems to be peculiar to the territory."[228]

Somehow, however, Memphis managed to hold its homicides down to fifty-seven in 1925—twelve whites and forty-five Blacks. The city held its breath and felt that it could rightfully deny the "murder capital" title.[229] By 1927, the crisis seemed to be over. A New York insurance journal rated Chicago as the leader in 1926 homicides and did not even mention Memphis.[230] The time was not many years away, beginning around 1940, when Memphis would be considered one of the nation's quietest and most peaceful cities. The 1960s were to swing the pendulum back again.

CHAPTER 10

THE BUCKLE OF THE BIBLE BELT

The changes brought about by the twentieth century, the horrors of the world war and growing industrialism seem to have accentuated and encouraged a desire in many Americans during the '20s to seek the comfort and safety of the simple fundamentals of the Bible.[231] Memphis was no exception.

In February 1924, folk dances and square dances were to be held one night at a meeting of Girl Scouts in the Columbian Mutual Hall in Memphis. Before the dances could be held, however, the Protestant Pastors Association met and opposed any form of dance being held in the name of the Girl Scouts. The Girl Scouts held their meeting, but the dances were renamed, with some ingenuity, "rhythmic games."[232] Later in the year, the Shelby County Baptist Association, at the closing session of its annual convention, condemned the (whites-only) municipal swimming pool and dance pavilion at the Fairgrounds for "frequent violations of the rules of decency." Reverend C.C. McCoy called the pool a "hell hole."[233]

Evangelism, or "orgiastic religion" as W.J. Cash called it, seemed to grow in the South in proportion to the disillusionment of poor whites with the industrialization of their society.[234] Memphis generously received evangelists during this era, and in the spring of 1924, it played host to the most famous of them all, Billy Sunday. Sunday was met at the train station by Mayor Paine and one hundred local clergymen and laymen. The evangelist reminisced about the baseball games he had played in Memphis some twenty-five years before, when he was a professional player. The only sin he could recall in the

Mayor Paine greets evangelist Billy Sunday and his wife. *Hooks Memphis Public Library.*

Memphis of those days was whiskey. On another occasion, he is supposed to have said that he did not know "any more about theology than a jack rabbit knows about pingpong."[235]

To accommodate Sunday's revival services, a large, barn-like "tabernacle" had been erected near the riverfront on the west side of Front Street at Jefferson, with an intended capacity of eight thousand. On the first night, twenty-five thousand people, "like an army terrible with banners," crowded into the tabernacle until it could hold no more. Hundreds milled about outside. All were white, as Blacks were to attend special meetings of their own.

The collection that night reached $2,655 (perhaps $30,000 today) for one service, and the crowd got its money's worth. Sunday treated the onlookers to the vigorous form of preaching for which he was noted. During the evening, he tore off his coat, smashed a chair to emphasize his contempt for Russia, leaped on a table, pounded the ceiling with his fist and dared the Devil to "seven weeks combat in an open field." He attacked modernism, evolution, pacifism, Bolshevism, "mummified churches," "ecclesiastical crooks," "the renaissance of jazz and junk" and the general deviltry of the world. He demanded that his listeners "drive the infidels and evolutionists out of the pulpit as traitors. Take this dirty, rotten evolution stuff out of schools and colleges supported by public money. Let the atheists build their own schools."

At another point, he chided his listeners, saying that "[an angel could not] come down and stay here two weeks and train with the crowd that some of you go with and call good and then go back to heaven without having a bath in Lysol and carbolic acid and formaldehyde."[236]

Perhaps as a gesture directed at the then-active Ku Klux Klan, Sunday pointedly refused to criticize Catholics and praised the Jews. Once started on his "sermon," Sunday disliked any sort of interruption. When a train passing along the track below the tabernacle hissed, Sunday snapped to his manager, "See the Illinois Central about that."

Most Protestant churches encouraged their members to attend Sunday's services. Eighty-six thousand people heard him the first week.[237] In early May, it was reported that Sunday had been stricken by a "fever" and was forced to call off the rest of his Memphis appearances. He soon left by train for the Mayo Clinic, taking the anxiety and prayers of thousands of Memphians with him, along with a personal fund of $20,130 ($280,000 today) raised in the city. Soon, Sunday was reported improved in Chicago.[238] He recovered and returned to Memphis in February 1925 for a two-week engagement at the Auditorium. His health was so robust, in fact, that he was able to join Sheriff Will Knight on a "still" raid in the Loosahatchie Bottoms. Sunday helped deputies run down three Black moonshiners and, viewing the mash, remarked, "That's hell brew sure enough. But won't the Devil be mad because we caught this still."[239]

The departure of the ailing Sunday in 1924 did not extinguish the evangelical flame burning in the Memphis area. Close on Sunday's heels came Gypsy Smith, another leading light of the sawdust trail to heaven. The crush of four thousand listeners forced the British-born evangelist of dulcet tones and polished speech to remove his orations to Sunday's recently vacated tabernacle on Front Street.[240] When Smith's four-day revival had run its course, the lesser-known Mel Trotter ("the rapid fire evangelist") came to town for a revival of whatever was left to revive.[241]

When it was all over, the *Commercial Appeal* made a saddening discovery: "The month of May, when a great religious revival was in a zenith of glory, produced the biggest crop of bootleggers, drunkards, gamblers, pistol toters, and vagrants, according to the docket at Police Headquarters, in a long, long, time."[242]

As the 1920s progressed, more and more speakers on religion incorporated attacks on the theory of evolution and its proponents in their sermons. Three-time presidential candidate and former secretary of state William Jennings Bryan came to Memphis in January 1925 to speak on both political and religious matters. In an address at the Court Avenue Presbyterian Church, and broadcast over the radio, Bryan attacked "modern" theologians, saying, "The Church is not greatly menaced today by the atheist of the outside, but is menaced today by the theistic evolutionist on the inside. They progressively dilute the word of God with scientific speculation until its authority is destroyed."[243] Bryan was the author of a "Weekly Bible Talks" syndicated column in many newspapers, including the *Commercial Appeal*.

A few days later, Bryan moved on to Nashville, where the Tennessee House of Representatives had just passed the Butler Act to prohibit the teaching of non-biblical theories of creation in public schools. The measure was, of course, aimed at the teaching of evolution. Bryan spoke in Nashville on his topic, "Is the Bible true?" His reply to his own question was that every word of it was. The speech was quickly printed and placed on the desk of every state senator. The Butler bill passed the senate and was reluctantly signed into law by Governor Austin Peay on March 21. It was a law that no branch of state government felt safe in opposing, no matter how little they personally cared for it.[244] This was a situation hardly novel in the annals of democratic government, especially in Tennessee.

When a young schoolteacher in the east Tennessee town of Dayton was persuaded to test the law's legality by violating it, the wheels were set in motion for the great summer spectacle of 1925 that has come to be known as the "Scopes trial." Later revelations by the local schemers indicated that there was not a little of the chamber of commerce mentality behind the testing of the law. Rhea County rushed to beat Chattanooga, which had a similar test case coming up. Nevertheless, to the defense of the Butler Act rushed legal forces led by William Jennings Bryan. The nation's attention focused on Tennessee and Dayton. The trial of Scopes for teaching evolution (from the official school text) was to start on July 10.[245]

Most Memphians had little sympathy with Scopes and the evolution forces, led by famed lawyer Clarence Darrow and American Civil Liberties counsel Dudley Field Malone. The *Commercial Appeal* called the ACLU "a radical organization which is always fighting something."[246] As for Scopes, they said, "The so-called scientist, who is an evolutionist, is a good deal like a slight [*sic*] of hand man at a country fair. The boys who look on know he is faking, but they just can't catch him and he walks away after the show is over, in form and gesture proudly eloquent."[247]

E.H. Crump had no doubt that the overwhelming majority of citizens in his end of the state favored the Butler Act. At that time, he was grooming the state treasurer, Hill McAlister, for the 1926 governor's race. He warned McAlister that Governor Peay was reaping all the glory and political benefit from the law and urged him to take "some of the play" away from Peay on the religious issue.[248] He even telephoned McAlister during the trial to urge that he make a statement demanding that Darrow be run out of the state. McAlister declined.[249] Crump counted Catholics, Protestants, Jews, Klansmen and African Americans as opposed to evolution.[250]

Memphis merchants tended to use public interest in the trial to attract attention to their products. Hull Dobbs Ford agency ran an advertisement shortly before the trial with cartoon monkeys dancing about the page. "No Monkey Business Here!" was their promise, referring to the widespread misconception that evolution taught that man was descended from monkeys or apes. "You don't care a hoop what we think about monkeys and Darrow, and Bryan and H.G. Wells—what you want is service!"[251]

Shortly before the Scopes trial began, the Tennessee Bar Association convened for its annual meeting. In 1925, Memphis was the host city. At the suggestion of Knoxville lawyers, Clarence Darrow, newly arrived in Knoxville, had been invited to address the convention. On the first afternoon of the convention, however, it was decided that "his visit might be misunderstood" at that time, the trial being such a short time away. Bar Association president Lovick P. Miles of Memphis wired Darrow on June 24 and withdrew the invitation.[252] The convention was unable to avoid controversy, however. On July 3, a Memphis attorney named Robert S. Keebler, born in east Tennessee, was given the floor for thirty minutes. Keebler was the grandson of a Methodist minister and was himself a Sunday school teacher at St. John's Methodist Church in Memphis. Confusion spread among the lawyers as Keebler attacked the Butler Act as a violation of the state constitution's command to cherish science and uphold religious and intellectual freedom. He offered a resolution of like effect. At the end of his original time allotment, a general outcry forced president Miles to allow Keebler fifteen additional minutes. Rebuttal arguments were demanded. An onlooker wrote, "To describe accurately the drama—or the comedy, if one chooses—of the scene which the Keebler address created is not within the power of words, printed or spoken. The eye and ear alone could grasp it. Bedlam was only mild confusion compared to it."

When the dust settled, Keebler's resolution was voted down 86–53 as a "religious discussion" and therefore out of order. Some lawyers yelled, "Let's eat!" The speech was expunged from the minutes.[253] Keebler subsequently resigned as a Sunday school teacher when he was accused of causing dissension in the church, and hints of heresy charges were discussed.[254]

When the Scopes trial finally ended with the hollow conviction of Scopes, it was Keebler whom the Bar Association named to thank the out-of-state lawyers for their interest and labors.[255] The trial in Dayton had taken on a carnival aspect, and Darrow's attacks on Fundamentalism's weaknesses had brought much ridicule to Tennessee. There was evidence when it was over that many Tennesseans felt it better to forget the Butler Act and make light of the trial. When Representative Butler introduced another bill, this time to outlaw gossip, the *Commercial Appeal* insisted that "what Tennessee needs is better laws and fewer of them."[256]

E.H. Crump took an urbane view of the trial the next year when, discussing the Philadelphia Sesquicentennial celebration of the Declaration of Independence, he wondered what sort of exhibit Tennessee could furnish: "Probably it would not cost very much to build a booth and put Scopes in it; provide a camp chair for Alvin York; exhibit a 5 gallon keg of Tate Springs water, and show a [Clarence Saunders] Sole Owner store."[257]

Fundamentalism survived in Memphis and surrounding rural areas but seemed to have lost some of its compulsion toward exhibitionism and involvement in political affairs for the time being.

CHAPTER 11

MEMPHIS AND PROHIBITION

The prohibition of the sale and possession of liquor, which became legal nationally in 1920, had been the law in Tennessee since 1909.[258] Memphis had never been very vigorous in its enforcement of the prohibition laws, especially during the administration of E.H. Crump as mayor. Mayor Crump had frankly stated that he did not believe in compulsory prohibition for large cities and had been ousted from the office of mayor for failure to enforce that law.

From 1909 to March 1, 1914, the prohibition law seems to have been entirely ignored in Memphis. Saloons were recognized and, in a measure, regulated by the city officials. The police knew of the conditions but made no effort to enforce the liquor laws. On the contrary, they recognized the existence of the saloons and assumed to regulate them by requiring that they close each night at midnight and that they remained closed all day Sunday. This condition continued and the saloons were not disturbed until March 1, 1914, when the state Nuisance Act went into effect. After this began a period during which the only effort to enforce the law was through injunction suits against purveyors of liquor, filed by the district attorney general or special counsel employed by the state government. The city authorities still did nothing. Several hundred injunction bills were filed and granted by the courts, a great many places closed and a large number of dealers were sent to the workhouse for violating the injunctions. However, intoxicating liquors continued to be sold in many places in the city, in varying degrees of openness. There was some effort at concealment and secrecy to guard against surprise by the special attorney in charge of the injunction suits and the officer working under him. But the saloons did not need to worry about danger from any other source. Some places maintained bars, and others did not. In many places, liquor was served in the rear of barbershops, restaurants and small grocery stores. In some parts of town, lunch counters were used as blinds, and in others, sales were made behind interstate shipping house signs. The main difference had become that the stocks of liquor were not kept conspicuously displayed but were kept more or less concealed or where they could be quickly removed. This condition existed until around February 1, 1915, and Sheriff J.H. Riechman (and Mayor Crump) did nothing toward enforcing the liquor laws in the city of Memphis except to serve the court papers in the injunction cases (which was the regular duty of a sheriff in any event). There were, however, a number of roadhouses and other places outside the city where liquor was being sold. These he seemed to have endeavored to break up. He had his deputies make a number of raids, arrest a good many people and destroy a considerable quantity of liquor. Also through his deputies, he secured indictments of a considerable number of persons for selling liquors outside the city. On February 1, 1915, the "Ouster Law," allowing the removal by courts of government officers not enforcing the law, went into effect. Immediately, the sheriff and city officials held a conference. Mayor Crump made a public statement that he was going to enforce the liquor laws, and the sheriff made a similar pronouncement. For a short time, an attempt at enforcement seems to have been made in Memphis. However, soon after the passage of the Ouster Law, the policy of enforcing the law through injunction suits was abandoned, and nothing further was done in that line except to wind up the suits already commenced.

Around May 1, 1915, the city officials adopted a new policy. Through the police, lists were made of all the places in the city in which it was known that liquor was being sold. Each dealer was arrested, but if he would turn over to the arresting officer a "forfeit" of fifty dollars, he and his saloon were left undisturbed. If he did not appear in city court, his fifty dollars was forfeited to the city, and that was the end of the matter. If he appeared, he was fined five dollars. In neither event was there an attempt to bind him over to the grand jury for a full-scale trial. There was obviously an understanding between the law enforcement officials and the liquor sellers. Under this plan, Memphis again had fairly open saloons. In places there was still some secrecy, and some places were being run in violation of injunctions and precautions had to be taken. Others were selling "on the sly" and trying to avoid paying an occasional forfeit of fifty dollars to the city. But there were a great many open saloons. The only exception to the sheriff's enforcement of the liquor laws outside the city limits was in the case of the Tri-State Fair (the whites-only fair, later known as the Mid-South Fair). In late August 1914, Sheriff Riechman met with Mayor Crump and the chief of police of Memphis and agreed, at Crump's request, to allow liquor at the fair if its directors were in favor of it. Apparently they were, for beer and whiskey were sold openly on the grounds during the fair, even while the sheriff was present.

Conditions tightened up somewhat when Crump was ousted from office as mayor by the chancery court for failure to enforce prohibition, and the federal Prohibition law was made effective in 1921. The days of the open saloon were, therefore, gone in Memphis by the 1920s.[259] However, despite reform movements, patriotic sentiment stirred by World War I and sporadic official attempts at enforcement, liquor was available at innumerable speakeasies and blind tigers in Memphis throughout the Prohibition era. The occasional raid on a secret saloon or blind tiger by police was usually due to failure of the owner to keep up his payments to the police or some political campaign fund. As in the rest of the urban nation, Prohibition simply was not popular with the majority of the people.[260] By 1924, federal authorities rated Tennessee 90 percent dry but considered Memphis the biggest Prohibition problem in the state. Bootleggers, both Black and white, did a thriving business importing liquor into the city for its thirsty citizens. Equipped with fast boats and operating from refuges among the islands in the Mississippi River, the motorized and water-going bootleggers were blamed by federal officials for most of the booze problem in Memphis. Stills hidden in safe spots along the river were a problem, as was an ingenious and elusive floating distillery that shifted its base of operations frequently. On one occasion, a rival mob dynamited whiskey-laden boats parked on the river right under the windows of the post office and federal court building. The *Commercial Appeal* considered stills within the county to be the major source of local liquor.[261]

Memphians seeking an evening of jazz music, dancing and free-flowing liquor were likely to seek out a roadhouse or nightclub on the outskirts of the city. One of these was Joe Baretta's place on Pigeon Roost Road (later Lamar), where one thousand gallons of wine were seized in a raid in 1925, after the noise of a party caused rural neighbors to call the sheriff.[262] Was Prohibition a failure? The *Commercial Appeal* did not think so. It blamed "a certain class of foreigners" for violations of the law and believed that Prohibition at least made it so hard for the poor to get liquor that they were

District Attorney General Tyler McLain. *Memphis Bar Association.*

forgetting about it.[263] It was true that prices had been pushed very high on bonded whiskey, but a local product such as "white lightning" was, fortunately or unfortunately, affordable by the poor.[264]

Local enforcement of Prohibition became very big news in the summer of 1927 with the exposure of the "Bellomini Green Book Scandal," which was to cause even the *New York Times* to take notice.[265] In the spring of 1927, federal Prohibition agents raided the bootleg "store" of John Bellomini at Butler and Fourth Streets in Memphis.[266] What made their raid unusual was the discovery of a little green book, a day ledger, containing the names of fifty-one city policemen, four deputy sheriffs and a handful of constables listed under the Italian word *legge* (meaning "law"). Opposite the names appeared sums of money from $5 to $20.[267] The total has been said to have been $84,000.[268] Mayor Rowlett Paine and police commissioner Thomas Allen called for investigation of the matter by federal judge Harry Anderson and U.S. Justice Department agents.[269] The federal district attorney's office hesitated, and the state district attorney general for Shelby County, William Tyler McLain, a member of the Crump organization, claimed that it would be "asinine" for the federal authorities to investigate the scandal, since it was a state matter.[270]

A city election was nearing, with Mayor Paine pitted against the Crump organization. Paine hinted that the local attorney general's office would whitewash the case if it got control of it and called again for federal action.[271] At this point, federal judge Harry Anderson, a Republican, properly pointed out that investigation was not up to him but to the United States district attorney. Commissioner Allen called Bellomini in for questioning while Mayor Paine sought an independent federal investigation from Washington. Several police officers were promoted from the ranks by Allen to form a special team to hit bootlegging and gambling throughout the city. Suspensions of suspected police officers began.[272]

Working in secret with Mayor Paine's knowledge, Commissioner Allen, U.S. district attorney Lindsey Phillips and federal Prohibition agent Alvin Howe began investigating the matter themselves. Bellomini was grilled again, for two hours. Finally, federal arrest warrants charging Bellomini and Joseph Rinaldi with conspiracy to violate the Prohibition laws were obtained. Two of Bellomini's alleged partners, Marico Vanucci and Dino Chiochetti, were sought but were found to have taken up residence in Italy.[273]

With Bellomini in custody, attention was turned to the suspected officers. Allen, convinced of the green book's authenticity, questioned Bellomini's African American employees and another partner, Alan McNamara, who was pardoned by Governor Peay in exchange for his cooperation. Thirty-eight officers were then suspended, including Captain Will Lee, in whose district Bellomini's "store" was located. Lee, later to become chief of police under the Crump organization, charged Allen with playing politics. Among those suspended

Federal judge Harry B. Anderson. *Memphis Bar Association*.

were many who would become well known in police matters in the 1930s, 1940s and 1950s, when Crump controlled the city. They included future chief Lee Quianthy and future inspectors Frank Glisson, John Foppiano and W.J. Raney (who later gained another kind of fame when he was in on the capture of "Machine Gun Kelly," a Memphian and kidnapper).[274]

The federal grand jury met and indicted Bellomini for operating a still at Black Fish Lake, Arkansas, and the retail outlet at Butler and Fourth.[275] The Shelby County grand jury took no action.[276] Upon his guilty plea, Bellomini was sentenced in federal court to six months in jail and a $1,000 fine.[277] The police officers were tried before a police trial board that heard the evidence on Bellomini's operation from his former minions. It seems that the liquor was stored in "cabins" near the store, from whence it was taken for distribution by white and Black bootleggers and drivers. Uniformed policemen and detectives often dropped in to call headquarters but were never seen to take a bribe. The store had been raided on occasion. A white employee testified that Chiochetti or Vanucci directed him to write the various names in the book for payoffs, but he did not write in the amounts.[278] The police officers admitted that they knew that the store was a "dive" and had raided it but claimed they had found little evidence of wrongdoing. They denied ever taking bribes.[279] On October 17, 1927, a matter of days before the city election that would oust Paine, the trial board found all officers not guilty.[280]

The "Green Book Scandal" was another example of the unwholesome situation that Prohibition had fostered in larger cities throughout the nation. Police officials, unwilling to enforce an unpopular law, were sometimes enmeshed in an unholy and hypocritical alliance with the lawbreakers. The exposure of this situation in Memphis resulted merely in creating a temporary political issue and brought about no change in the situation. Bootlegging continued under the auspices of enterprising African Americans and whites. Most of the suspended policemen were reinstated subsequently.[281] In 1928, police "discovered" a huge distillery on the second floor of a vacant garage at 285 Poplar, only four blocks from police headquarters. It consisted of a copper still, bumper and cookers of nine-hundred-gallon capacity set on a cement foundation, surrounded by a brick oven and six large wooden vats. Apparently, its existence was not properly accounted for, because it was hacked to pieces by the authorities.[282]

CHAPTER 12

CLARENCE SAUNDERS

I n 1904, a young man named Clarence Saunders moved to Memphis. He was to keep the city fascinated for most of the next fifty years. Saunders was as clever and flamboyant in the business sphere as Crump was in the political. Born to a poor family in Virginia, he was only thirty-nine as the '20s began but already a millionaire. He began working in a grocery as a boy and eventually became an entrepreneur in the wholesale and retail ends of the business. Acquaintances characterized him as both a man "of limitless imagination and energy" and "arrogant and conceited as all get out." They also regarded him as "essentially a four-year-old child, playing at things." His public behavior, which must have amused Memphians mightily, seemed to bear out the youthful appellation. He made his first fortune through clever advertising and the brilliantly simple idea of making grocery stores self-service. The national chain of low-price grocery stores that he soon headed was called Piggly-Wiggly in order to arouse interest and curiosity.

In 1923, in an attempt to prevent stock manipulators from forcing down the value of Piggly-Wiggly stock, Saunders borrowed huge sums and put in wholesale orders for shares at inflated prices, knowing that the manipulators could not obtain the stock within the time allowed by the New York Stock Exchange. Unfortunately for Saunders, the exchange suspended its rules, allowing the manipulators to make delivery. Saunders had to make out a check (on the corporation) for $1,600,000. The directors of the Piggly-Wiggly Corporation were less than pleased by the fiasco, and Saunders resigned.[283]

He filed for bankruptcy in February 1924, when it was alleged that the money he borrowed was taken for his own account, rather than that of the Piggly-Wiggly Corporation. He listed assets of $3,244,070 and debts of $1,976,919. His assets included a townhouse with swimming pool (later the University Club) and the vast, unfinished country estate Cla-Le-Clare (now Chickasaw Gardens and the Pink Palace museum). He was already planning a new chain of stores.[284]

With typical ballyhoo, in the literary style that was to puzzle and delight Memphians for decades, Saunders placed a full-page advertisement in the newspaper on March 6, 1924, to announce the opening the next day of his first new "democratic but clean" store at Third and Madison Streets:

> *Faith and more faith, purified by wisdom with my eye-teeth fully developed, entitles me to smile unreservedly and clasp your hand warmly. Come and let's have a good and glorious time!...Furious are some because the bankrupt won't die and dry up. To them it is not enough that they have all my money and possessions....Complete annihilation is the only full satisfaction for them....'Tis the throng of the unafraid and confident men and women who are waiting with expectancy this new store. They believe in me and to them I signal with a flaming torch, burning into the future these letters: "Success."...*[signed] *Clarence Saunders Stores System.*[285]

As was his custom, Saunders stood for ten hours straight at the doorway of his new store, handing out carnations as jazz bands played for the customers. Twenty to twenty-five thousand visitors came to the store, which differed from the Piggly-Wiggly chiefly in its lack of turnstiles and rearrangement of shelves.[286]

The directors of the Piggly-Wiggly Corporation quickly sought to enjoin Saunders from operating his new store, alleging that he had sold the corporation all rights and patents to such self-service stores, as well as the benefit of the publicity that attached to the "Clarence Saunders Self-Service" name.[287] The injunction was temporarily granted, and Saunders took to the newspapers, denying that he had sold or had the right to sell exclusive rights to the self-service concept. As for selling his *name*, his position was clearly established in the advertisement's signature: "Clarence Saunders. Sole Owner of This name."[288] On March 30, federal judge William Ross agreed with Saunders's position, and a triumphant advertisement appeared the next day: "Wash Day is here!...Farewell to the old as I embrace for all time the New day."[289]

The store reopened to throngs of customers. Litigation between Piggly-Wiggly and Saunders went on for years, but by January 1926, there were 102 Clarence Saunders, Sole Owner of My Name stores throughout the South, (soon dubbed Sole Owner stores), providing him a new fortune.[290]

Saunders's most lasting contribution to Memphis was the estate that he was building on the outskirts of the city on Central Avenue. On the gently rolling acres of Cla-Le-Clare rose a salmon-pink stone mansion, known by Memphians ever since as "the Pink Palace." Before the house was completed, Saunders was bankrupt.[291] Leading citizens urged Mayor Paine to have the city purchase the estate for school or park property. The mayor declined, pointing to the Fairgrounds and Galloway Park nearby.[292] There were rumors that the land might be sold for a cemetery[293] and that the Pink Palace would be leveled.[294] The land was sold in 1925 by the trustee in bankruptcy for $343,252 (perhaps $5,000,000 today) to some local businessmen.[295] A few months later, the Garden Communities Corporation and Harland Bartholomew, a professional city planner, announced that the Cla-Le-Clare estate would become Chickasaw Gardens, a planned, "restricted" "garden community," modeled on those elsewhere in America

Cla-Le-Clare (later the Pink Palace museum) nearing completion. *Hooks Memphis Public Library*.

Clarence Saunders relaxes at his new country home, later Lichterman Nature Center. *Hooks Memphis Public Library.*

and England.[296] The Georgia marble of the Pink Palace had not all been put into place by its imported Scottish stonemasons when the mansion slipped through Saunders's hands. Subsequently, the city acquired and completed the building and turned it into the city museum.[297]

Saunders threw himself into politics with the same reckless energy that he showed in his business dealings. He defied "Boss" Crump on more than one occasion, supporting Austin Peay for governor when Crump was grooming another candidate.[298] With the Great Depression of the 1930s went the last of Saunders's great fortunes. He never gave up inventing ingenious new marketing devices, but somehow, they never met with real success.[299] The times were somehow no longer right. It would probably not be entirely accurate to say that Clarence Saunders was a product of his era. He had a personal ingenuity and *élan* that undoubtedly contributed to the success he achieved. It seems clear, however, that his rapid success came in an era particularly favorable to a combination of easily obtained investment capital, ballyhoo and more efficient methods of marketing. By the time of his second fall, in 1931, he was no longer a business novelty. For Memphians, however, he was one of those flamboyant figures who has become a local legend.

CHAPTER 13

NOSTALGIA

For all its physical growth and enthusiasm for material progress, Memphis, like most southern cities, maintained its attachment to the romantic legend of the "Old South" and the noble "Lost Cause." Urban life, with its commercial bustle and mass modernization, accentuated the sense of nostalgia by white Memphians for the more leisurely (for them), idyllic Old South and its supposedly more noble ideals. By 1912, the southern legends of slavery days and Reconstruction were popular even in the North.[300] Ignoring feeble protests, the pioneering film *The Birth of a Nation* (depicting an idealized, racist view of the Civil War and Reconstruction) played to enthusiastic and packed houses throughout the country in 1915–16 and had an extended run in Memphis.[301] But sometime between 1912 and the mid-1920s, a kind of "neo-abolitionist" image of the South, spurred by journalists and writers, both within and without the region, seriously threatened the legends.[302] Smarting from this dual attack on a dream that they held dear, many white southerners assumed a protective, defensive attitude toward the past. Southern newspapers from time to time carried articles lamenting the deaths of elderly African Americans who fitted the stereotype of the loyal plantation servant. On some occasions, journalists went to almost ludicrous lengths to defend the past. When a previously unpublished 1858 speech by Abraham Lincoln, pleading against the extension of slavery beyond the borders of slave states, was uncovered, the *Commercial Appeal* hopefully headlined that the speech "Favored Toleration of Slavery."[303]

Physically, too, the vestiges of the Old South were passing gradually into history. From 1812, when Robert Fulton sent the Mississippi River its first steamboat, through the halcyon antebellum days when Mark Twain was a river pilot, the riverboat was a vital part of the South's life. By the 1850s, some five hundred steamboats plied the river, picking up cotton at plantation docks, depositing it at markets like Memphis or New Orleans and otherwise carrying the cargoes and people that the railroads had not yet reached. In 1870, Memphians crowded the bluffs to witness the famous race between the steamers *Natchez* and *Robert E. Lee*.[304] By 1924, Memphis still had packet boats, mostly sternwheelers, tied at its riverfront. The two remaining Memphis riverboat lines as 1924 began were the Lee Line and the Delta Line. The boats they operated from Memphis were the *Kate Adams*, the *Harry Lee*, the *Eclipse*, the *Verne Swain*, the *Dixie* and the *Princess*. The famous Lee Line had started in 1866 when James Lee Sr. established his first steamers from Memphis to Friars Point, Mississippi, just south of Memphis. Railroads and motor trucks took business away from the riverboats steadily every year by the twentieth century. For a while, the two steamer lines were able to continue operations with some success by making an agreement to maintain rates and avoid competing with each other. The area of the river between Greenville, Mississippi, and Caruthersville, Missouri, was divided between the two lines. Then came a disagreement between them and a price-cutting war. The result, in January 1924, was the sale of the two lines to the Valley Line, a corporation owned by Captain Peters Lee and Captain Tom Rees. The Valley Line defaulted on payments of the purchase price in July 1925, however, and the boats were attached in federal court in early 1926. Mail to Corona, Dean's Island, Reverie, Fulton and Prestige, Tennessee, still carried by packet, was temporarily halted. On the evening of January 2, 1926, the Valley Line boats tied up, banked their fires, released their roustabouts and ceased operations. For the first time in its history, the *Commercial Appeal* asserted sadly, Memphis had no river packet.[305]

In the summer of 1924, after a great deal of anticipation, Memphis was host to that embodiment of southern nostalgia, a reunion of Confederate veterans. The biggest load of veterans arrived in Memphis on June 4. The hot evening was cooled by a summer rain as fifteen special trains converged on Memphis. The new Auditorium was headquarters for the reunion, and it was there that the aging soldiers were welcomed by the ubiquitous Mayor Paine, himself the son of a Confederate veteran. These former defenders of their beloved Lost Cause were old men now, most in their eighties. They were helped about by Boy Scouts, and merchants on the west side of Main

Confederate reunion parade, Main Street, 1924. *University of Memphis Special Collections.*

Street near the Auditorium put out chairs for them. The *Commercial Appeal* seemed moved by the fragility of the old fighters and urged the citizenry to take care of them during their stay. Fourteen of the visitors, old and overtired from their trip, were taken to the hospital. Nevertheless, 3,500 had registered for the reunion by the evening of June 3.[306]

Many of the veterans were billeted in Billy Sunday's "tabernacle" on Front Street at Jefferson, and a Texan died there shortly after his arrival.[307] A parade of veterans in their gray uniforms, along with floats and bands, enlivened the proceedings and moved the *Commercial Appeal* to rhapsodize: "Onward and onward. These soldiers of a beloved cause, exultant and triumphant, carried their colors and their glory as thousands paid homage to their valor and their faith."[308]

Not everyone was sentimental about the Civil War. One old Rebel, age eighty-four, was heard to remark as he rested on a bench near Sunday's tabernacle: "By golly, that was a nasty war, wasn't it? There at Shiloh we were fightin' and a-knockin' and a-stabbin' like fury—I stuck lots of them durned Yankees with my bayonet. We got lots of 'em that day—and they got lots of us."[309]

Not all of those at the reunion fit the romantic image of aging aristocrats of vanished wealth. One day during the convention, four white-haired veterans, dressed in their gray uniforms, sat alone on their kit bags in front of the massive classical stone façade of Union Station. These former defenders of the Lost Cause were conspicuous among the other arrivals because they were African Americans. Detective Inspector W.T. Griffin, making his rounds, spotted the quartet and, after some inquiries, was told that they wanted to go register for the convention. A police car was summoned to the curb, and they all got in. Up Beale Street the car went. "Been hearin' about this street for forty years," said one of the four. The newspaper quoted another as saying, "Sure is a lot o' niggers lives along here." Beale Streeters were said to have gaped at the gray-clad four on the back seat of the squad car. Up Main Street the car went, asserting its right of way over other traffic, as traffic cops smiled and pedestrians stared. Safely at the Auditorium, Griffin placed his charges in the hands of Boy Scouts. "Wouldn't know what to do without my white folks," Ruben Henderson, eighty-eight, is supposed to have said (for publication, at least) as he thanked the inspector. The others echoed him. They had come from Florence and Huntsville, Alabama, and Blacksburg, South Carolina, sponsored by "their white folks." Henderson was reported to have been a veteran of the Fifth Alabama Infantry (although in what capacity was not stated) and displayed documents to prove that he had attended every reunion except one. "Best

Union Station. *Hooks Memphis Public Library.*

fun I've had in a long time," chuckled Inspector Griffin patronizingly, as he headed back to headquarters.[310] Sharing the attention with the four was "Uncle" Steve Eberhart, who had followed two Rome, Georgia men through the war and who, according to the reporter, "strutted his feathers" at all the reunions. The men's true roles in the war were suggested when he was dubbed by the other veterans as "the champion chicken chaser of the Confederacy."[311]

The reunion reached its climax on the evening of June 6, with a grand ball at the Auditorium attended by eighteen thousand (white) people. Another milestone had been reached. The remnants of the army of the Confederacy disbanded once again, its ranks growing thinner even as its legend grew.[312]

CHAPTER 14

THE SILENT MINORITY

I n 1860, African Americans (most, but not all, slaves) constituted only 17 percent of the population of Memphis. In 1920, they constituted 38 percent. Between those two dates, Blacks, impelled at first by their newly won freedom and, later, by the depressed condition of agriculture in the surrounding region, moved to Memphis in large numbers.[313] For most of them, the city would mean work and a better life, including a vestige of political power.[314] They had been allowed to vote in Memphis for years, even in the days when other sections of the South were progressively restricting their rights. In reality, however, the African American franchise in Memphis represented little political power. If Black votes were needed in an election, the required number of Blacks would usually be "voted" by one white political faction or another to the accompaniment of anguished cries by the opposition.[315]

One of the most frequent charges in Memphis politics, especially in regard to the Crump forces, was that "hordes" of African Americans were being "voted." Of course, the word "hordes" is subject to various interpretations. It is interesting to note, however, that comparatively few citizens of either race voted in Shelby County in the 1920s. In the 1924 county election, for example, 50,000 persons, representing only 27 percent of the adults of voting age in the county registered to vote. Of this number, only 26,400, or 14 percent of those eligible troubled to actually vote.[316] As for the Black vote in Memphis, statistics on the four wards most heavily populated by Blacks and the returns from those wards in the 1924, 1926 and 1927 elections are instructive. The following figures are compiled from the 1920 federal census and from reported election returns:

GENERAL STATISTICS

Population of Shelby County in 1924	223,216
Memphis adults of voting age in 1920	107,868
Memphis white adults of voting age in 1920	65,709
Memphis "colored" adults of voting age in 1920	42,159
Registered voters in Shelby County in 1924	50,000
Shelby County votes cast in 1924 election	26,400
Registered voters in Shelby County in 1926	44,000
Shelby County votes cast in 1926 election	19,633
Votes cast in Memphis in 1924 election	19,671
Votes cast in Memphis in 1927 election	27,926

VOTING IN THE LEADING BLACK WARDS[317]

THIRTY-FIFTH WARD (HORN LAKE ROAD AREA)

Eligible whites (1920)	271
Eligible Blacks (1920)	801
Total eligible (1920)	1,072
Total vote for mayor in 1923 election	339
Votes for Taylor in 1923	62
Total vote for governor in 1926 Democratic primary	339
Votes for Peay in 1926 Democratic primary	16
Total vote for mayor in 1927 election	352
Votes for Paine in 1927	10

ELEVENTH WARD (WELLINGTON-GEORGIA AREA)

Eligible whites (1920)	1,211
Eligible Blacks (1920)	3,174
Total eligible (1920)	4,385
Total vote for mayor in 1924 primary	303
Votes for Taylor in 1924	80
Total vote for governor in 1926 election	237
Votes for Peay in 1926	15
Total vote for mayor in 1927 election	619
Votes for Paine in 1927 election	48

TWENTY-FOURTH WARD (FLORIDA STREET AREA)

Eligible whites (1920)	962
Eligible Blacks (1920)	2,791
Total eligible (1920)	3,753
Total vote for mayor in 1923 election	352
Votes for Taylor in 1924	83
Total vote for governor in 1926 Democratic Primary	248
Votes for Peay in 1926	25
Total vote for mayor in 1927 election	386
Votes for Paine in 1927	15

FIFTH WARD (BEALE STREET)

Eligible whites (1920)	2,057
Eligible Blacks (1920)	3,201
Total eligible (1920)	5,258
Total vote for mayor in 1923 election	501
Votes for Taylor in 1924	41
Total vote for governor in 1926 Democratic primary	551
Votes for Peay in 1926 Democratic primary	17
Total vote for mayor in 1927 election	402
Votes for Paine in 1927	30[318]

Once again, except perhaps, for the Thirty-Fifth Ward, the most striking thing about the figures is that they demonstrate how few citizens of either race voted. It is clear, however, that very few eligible Black Memphians cast a ballot. The "hordes" of Black voters, if they existed, were comparative to some low standard fixed in the protestant's mind. It is interesting to note that, in each of the elections, the anti-Black (and anti-Crump) candidate was overwhelmingly defeated in those Black wards. The greatest increase in voting (except in the Fifth Ward) occurred in the 1927 city election, in which, as we shall see, Black leadership threw its support to the Crump forces in the face of Mayor Paine's overt white supremacy platform.[319]

Various reasons have been advanced for the low voting turnout in Shelby County, the most logical being the restriction caused by the biennial registration and the $2.10 poll tax required by state law.[320] African American voters in Memphis were doubtless politically useful when properly organized and could be used effectively in close races, their poll tax receipts being supplied by enterprising ward heelers. Their increased voting activity in the 1927 city race indicates that a concerted Crump campaign to win their votes, and a desire to repudiate white supremacy attacks, could move them to increased turnout at the polls. That, despite their apparent reluctance to assert themselves in the white man's elections.[321]

The feeling that African Americans were better off in the cities, and especially in Memphis, was shared by many. Taking stock in 1924 of the racial situation in the South, the Reverend Sutton E. Griggs, a Black Memphian and pastor, wrote that the "Negro" was steadily making progress. He pointed out that economic progress was the key to all other kinds and noted that in the South, Blacks had a monopoly on "sun jobs," in which they did not have to compete with "one of the most vigorous and aggressive types of men—i.e. the sun-shy Nordic type." Blacks in the North were not so fortunate, he thought. Reverend Griggs felt that in Memphis, Blacks came nearer to penetrating the whole field of industry than in any other city in the country.

The American Car and Foundry Company employed four hundred Black Memphians at from $2.50 ($35.00 today) to $7.00 a day to do steel erection work. "They are preferred to foreign help," it was noted. The Frisco Railroad shops and the Illinois Central Railroad freight house each employed around two hundred Black Memphians at salaries up to $5.00 a day. The Memphis Terminal Corporation, employing six hundred, reported good relations with its Black employees except for two men "led off by a bad element." The forty engaged at the Edgar-Morgan Feed Company all carried life insurance for $500.00 at ten cents a week. Orgill Brothers employed seventy-five in its wholesale hardware business and gave a year's salary to the widow of each twenty-year veteran.

Of more interest was the fact that Memphis had two banks owned by African Americans in 1924, with aggregate resources of $1,380,000, and two insurance companies employing 750 persons. A Black casket company was valued at $200,000 ($3 million today) and was paying dividends of 7 percent. In all, "colored" wealth was figured at over $8 million ($100 million today), with half of that amount deposited in the various banks about town. There was one Black millionaire, two Black quarter-millionaires and thirteen more African American Memphians with substantial assets by anyone's standards.

Black Memphians had five private parks, four business colleges (which businesses they trained for is a matter of some conjecture), 107 churches (66 Baptist, 27 "Methodist"), twenty-five dentists, eight lawyers, eighty-six "physicians," eighty-seven barbershops, eight drugstores, two candy factories, sixteen blacksmith shops (plenty of horses and mules still pulling conveyances), four cemeteries, twenty-six boardinghouses, seventy-six groceries, 194

Melrose school for "colored." *Memphis Heritage.*

hairdressers, twenty music teachers, three newspapers, fifty-six shoemakers, fourteen funeral parlors, six hospitals and one eye-ear-nose-and-throat specialist physician. There were eighteen public grammar schools for them, with 275 teachers, as well as Howe and LeMoyne Institutes for more advanced study. The former enrolled 350 students but could boast a physical plant worth only $62,000 ($850,000 today). Howe was owned and controlled by African Americans but received annual contributions from whites. LeMoyne depended chiefly on northern benevolence and tuition to continue the education of its 436 students. The total faculty payroll was only $4,500.

Still, Reverend Griggs for one was optimistic. He found race relations cordial and even further progress being made. White citizens were building an orphanage for African Americans, lynching was quiescent in the state and, as has been noted, Memphis Blacks could vote. Reverend Griggs would not put a limit on the degree of success his people might attain working with the whites.[322]

Looking at other, more depressing statistics, we can see that the traditional southern activity of lynching Black people was falling off. It was reported that there were "only" 281 lynchings in the United States in the period from 1919 through 1929. This was half the number recorded in the previous decade, and in 1929, there were "only" 7 lynchings.[323] In retrospect, 281 mob murders hardly seems a number of which to be proud. And yet, even Tuskegee Institute, which recorded the statistics of lynchings, began to adopt the hopeful word "only."[324] When it was reported that "only" 16 persons (including 4 whites) had been lynched in 1924, the *Commercial Appeal* editorialized that it was glad that the problem was "being solved."[325]

If the problem was being solved, the reasons do not appear to have been entirely a change of racial attitudes by southern whites. It has been suggested that there was a feeling among the more influential whites that the African American was "mastered" safely and that the orderly processes of commerce should not be upset by uncontrolled violence.[326] The indications are that the basic emotional causes of lynching remained. Of over 1,600 Black lynchings in the period from 1900 through 1929, only 8 trials (of 54 persons) resulted in convictions in connection with the deaths. And in none of the convictions was the punishment commensurate with that normally expected in murder cases.[327] During the '20s, reports of lynchings from throughout the South, and especially in Mississippi, appeared in the *Commercial Appeal*. There were floggings[328] and burnings at the stake.[329] The Mississippi National Guard was needed to restore order in Gulfport, Mississippi, during a lynching riot.[330] A Black lunatic suspected of murder was beaten to death in Meridian, Mississippi.[331]

Shelby County, Tennessee, was not beyond such measures. In the fall of 1927, a white Barretville woman accused a twenty-eight-year-old Black man of trying to "assault" her but reported that she was able to drive him off with a hoe. A short time later, the man was seen at Paul Barret's store, where he borrowed five dollars and purchased a small quantity of clothing. Sheriff Knight began a search for the accused at once but was unsuccessful in locating him. The next morning, the man's body was found in a churchyard, riddled with bullets. The small bundle of clothes lay nearby. The sheriff swore to charge the killers with first-degree murder if he ever found them. He did not find them.[332]

The *Commercial Appeal* stoutly condemned lynching as uncivilized, but when, in 1924, Congress considered the Dyer Anti-Lynch Bill, the paper vehemently opposed its passage. The proposed law provided that the county of a lynching would pay the victim's relatives $10,000 and that the lynchers would be tried in federal, not state, court. The *Commercial Appeal* called the bill "one of the most brazen exhibitions of Republican hypocrisy ever staged in Congress" and listed its reasons for opposition:

> *It penalized the innocent of the county*
> *It violated the Fifth and Tenth amendments to the Constitution*
> *It made lynchings profitable*
> *It was election year politics*
> *Lynchings were declining anyway*[333]

The bill failed to pass, but two years later, NAACP lawyers, beginning a long legal struggle, attacked in the U.S. Supreme Court covenants in deeds restricting the sale of land to white persons.[334] Race was still firmly imbedded in the law.

White Memphians were not about to give up their traditional racial attitudes. When most of the African American soldiers from Memphis returned from military service in the world war in early 1919, they received much the same welcome as their white comrades in arms, although separately. There were separate parades and bands and speeches.[335] The war had not erased the patronizing attitude toward Black people that existed in the North as well as in the South.[336] In 1925, Lieutenant General Robert Bullard, in a syndicated news story, accused Black soldiers of cowardice in the "Great War," as the First World War was then called.[337] The strong reaction of Black people throughout the country, citing words of praise and decorations awarded to Black soldiers and units by several Allied nations, merely pointed to the fact that the racial problem was still very much alive.[338] The systematic and legalized segregation of the races had begun in earnest in the South in 1896 and had been completed by the time of America's entry into the world war. Separation of races had become an article of faith with white persons in the South, intertwined with the "myth of the Confederacy."[339] "What's the matter with the world, anyway?" asked E.H. Crump when Senator Thomas J. Walsh of Montana, a "crusader" whom he admired, ate catfish with Black people. Crump, like many Memphians, was a transplanted Mississippian.[340]

When three Black female nurses were hired to tend Black patients at the Memphis General Hospital because of the shortage of white nurses, the white interns met and threatened to quit. The white nurses joined in the protest, and the Black nurses were dismissed. It was then announced that the hospital would have to restrict its admissions due to crowding and shortage of nurses.[341] In a "revolutionary move" in 1925, the Claridge Hotel overnight replaced all of its Black bellhops with white boys, some from other towns. The manager explained that experience had taught the hotel that white boys "afforded better satisfaction to the general run of guests."[342]

One realizes how long ago 1924 was when one learns that in that year a "stir" was created both in Memphis and Washington, D.C., by the fact that an African American was in the U.S. Marine Corps. Ralph Wright of Memphis had enlisted and was believed to be the first Black man to do so. A marine general, identified only as "General Deland," reportedly commented that "there is no law against their enlistment, but they have been shown that they might not like the service."[343]

A notorious Saturday night practice of this period in Memphis, usually confined to sheriff's deputies acting under a justice of the peace, was to raid Black neighborhoods and make wholesale arrests. Sometimes homes were invaded without benefit of any legal process. Those arrested would then be brought before a justice, who would exact exorbitant "fees" and "costs" from the usually innocent victims.[344] City police, also, were not hesitant about arresting Black people, and almost any Monday morning would see city judge Clifford Davis's courtroom crowded with twenty-five to fifty African Americans, the sweepings of a weekend's police activity. The charges usually related to gambling and were disposed of expeditiously with two-dollar fines for those who pleaded guilty.[345] The minions of the justices of the peace seemed to conduct their raids with greater premeditation—and with greater profit. One such raid was also the source of this lyric report (demonstrating the general white attitude) by a long-forgotten *Commercial Appeal* reporter:

> *It was twilight along Beale Avenue. Senegambian syncopators were tuning up for the usual Sunday evening frolic. The first autumn breezes were blowing across the old Mississippi, wafting the odor of fried catfish and hamburger along the avenue Handy's "Beale Street Blues" made famous in Afro-American history.*
>
> *This is apple blossom time for Memphis Negroes, figuratively speaking—cotton picking season just ahead and a bumper crop in the fields. Beale Avenue already has sensed a period of prosperity on the way. Pee Wee's place, across from 314, was doing its usual Sunday night's business and languid strollers were starting out on their customary promenade. Back in 314, unseen from the front, the galloping dominoes were in motion, performing before a congregation of twenty-three Negroes. The bones were rolling with impunity across the silent cloth. Only murmurs could be heard from the entrance. "Six bits ah hit, niggah," ejaculated a tall high-brown, tossing three silver pieces into the ring. "Shoot yo head off," said another. Things were perking up and there were signs of an auspicious evening until—well—the last thing they expected to see was a posse of sheriff's deputies infringing on Mike Kehoe's popular indoor pastime—raiding Negro poolrooms. When Inspector Kehoe goes out for a stroll, Beale Avenue gives him plenty of room. But they didn't know anything about this sheriff's posse.[346]*

The posse herded up twenty-three people at 314 and took them to the county jail. Justice of the Peace Ed Bradley was called, and twenty-three

Beale Street, circa 1924. *Hooks Brothers.*

warrants were on their way. Justice Bradley's office was about two blocks from 314. The price was $12.50 per prisoner, including jail fees. They were accustomed to a club rate of $2.00 per head in Judge Clifford Davis's court. A similar raid had been staged on Pee Wee's place on Beale the day before, when nineteen Blacks were arrested and Judge Louis Morris taxed them $12.55 per head. The deputies had launched the "uplift" on Beale Avenue.[347] The *Commercial Appeal* likened the justices and their deputies to vultures "who feast…upon that element which can be scared into submission."[348] A squire and several deputies were indicted for extortion in 1924,[349] and the grand jury made another investigation in 1925,[350] but the practice was inherent in the system.

A river disaster in 1925 spotlighted an African American who was a hero to many white Memphians. Tom Lee, age forty-two, an employee of a firm that made willow matting to protect the riverbanks, was heading up the Mississippi River for Memphis on May 8, 1925, in his skiff *Zev* when he spied people in the water. They were the survivors of a group of engineers and their families who had been inspecting the river works in the sternwheeler *M.E. Norman* when it turned over and sank, drowning twenty. Lee saved thirty-two persons, landing them on the bank and on sandbars.[351] He quickly became a local hero and was even taken to the White House to be congratulated by President Coolidge. The *Commercial Appeal* immediately began a campaign

Top: Tom Lee, hero of the M.E. Norman sinking. *University of Memphis Special Collections*.

Bottom: On the White House lawn on May 28, 1925, President Coolidge honors Tom Lee, hero of the *M.E. Norman* sinking. *Library of Congress*.

to raise a fund for Lee, but donations were at first slow to come in. The goal was not reached until late July, when $3,025 ($40,000 today) was raised to buy Tom Lee a house. In October, a small house was purchased at 923 North Watkins, with three of those rescued by Lee named as trustees in the deed.[352] Lee moved in and lived there for the rest of his life. For many white Memphians, there was that patronizing old southern feeling of satisfaction in rewarding a faithful servant. It was not until the 1950s, however, after his death, that the city erected a small obelisk monument to Lee on the riverfront, on which he was described as "a very worthy Negro."

Perhaps Memphis African Americans looked to religion for understanding and protection. After all, had not revivalist Billy Sunday told some fifteen thousand of them that Christ was willing "to intercede for sinners whose hearts are white even if their skins are black"?[353]

In Memphis, an African American could make money and could vote. But he or she could not escape the white supremacy tradition that was firmly entrenched in Memphis as elsewhere in the South. The 1927 city elections, which will be discussed later, showed, however, that Black Memphians were not without some political influence in the community, and the repudiation of Rowlett Paine's white supremacy platform by the white voters demonstrated a certain reluctance on their part to adopt a hostile attitude in racial matters.

Memphis Blacks were not without their champions and heroes, especially in the political arena. The Republican Party was still the Black man's party in the South in the 1920s. Not until the 1980s would the Republican Party absorb the white southern Democrats and turn the "Solid South" from a

Bob Church Jr., W.C. Handy and Lieutenant George W. Lee in front of Church's Beale Street bank. *Hooks Brothers.*

Democratic stronghold into a Republican one. The leader of the Memphis Republicans in the 1920s was a wealthy African American banker and investor named Robert R. "Bob" Church Jr. Church had been born of a wealthy, famous father and was a Black aristocrat. He had studied at Oberlin College and observed the world of Wall Street. Every election year since 1912, he had been elected a delegate to the Republican National Convention.[354] Church had captured the attention and respect of Republican Party leaders such as Will Hays, the national chairman, when, in 1920, he refused to make a public issue at the national convention of whether his delegation or that of the white Republicans should represent Shelby County. In return for his cooperation, Church received from the Republican National Committee "certain promises that made his future in the Republican Party secure."[355] Church's political power consisted mainly of his right to pass upon or recommend federal political appointments during the years 1921–33, when Republicans sat in the White House. In 1928, the *Commercial Appeal* commented on Church's position:

> *No federal appointment is made in Memphis or in Shelby County under a Republican administration without his endorsement. Federal office holders and applicants for federal favor not only admit his authority but seek his favor....He is in the high councils of the party. Church is modest and unassuming. He never projects himself into the spotlight of local politics. His work is done in his Beale Street office in Memphis and in the White House in Washington....Church is the head of the Republican Party in this county. He ranks higher than* [east Tennessee GOP congressman] *J. Will Taylor in the state. His influence in the Republican Party is more extensive in the South than any man, white or black.*[356]

It is doubtful that Church exercised much control over the course of political affairs outside his local party group. He controlled few votes, even among Blacks, and he was constantly opposed by local "Lily-White" Republicans led by such men as Harry True and C. Arthur Bruce.[357] Republican congressman J. Will Taylor of east Tennessee controlled federal patronage in Tennessee, although he often deferred to Church's wishes.[358] Church's influence in federal circles seems to have come in large part from his unswerving loyalty to the party, coupled with his refusal to accept money or public office for himself.[359]

As 1924 opened, Church and his African American group were in danger of being excluded altogether from local Republican councils. The county and district committees were controlled by Harry True and Tom Taylor, respectively. At a meeting of the state committee in Nashville in January, Church managed to get agreement to one-third Black representation in the state convention.[360] There were 417 whites, almost all Ku Klux Klansmen, and 90 Blacks. Most of the whites were led by W. Joe Wood, who had run for mayor against Rowlett Paine in 1923. These "Lily-Whites" rejected the national committee's recommendation that a mixed delegation of whites and Blacks be elected, and the two groups split. Confusion reigned as the rival Republicans held their meetings in the same room at the same time. Predictably, the "Lily-Whites" elected an all-white delegation, while the Church-dominated faction elected a mixed slate.[361]

The Church forces had reached an understanding with district committee leader Tom Taylor, and the "Black and Tan" alliance sent two-thirds of the representation to the state convention in Knoxville, where they were recognized as the representatives of the regular party organization from the Tenth District. The "Lily-Whites" refused to participate further, and the convention delegates from the rest of the state chuckled at Shelby County's Republican politics.[362]

In the national Republican convention in Cleveland in the summer of 1924, Church's power and prestige among the GOP of his county and district was solidified by the seating of his delegation after a hard fight.[363] He suffered a setback shortly thereafter when the chancery court in Memphis ruled that the "Black and Tan" GOP primary board, which governed the Republican primary, was irregularly elected. They were therefore enjoined from acting, leaving the primary in the control of the incumbent "Lily-Whites."[364]

Church showed his influence in national party councils, however, when in 1924, "Lily-Whites" invited GOP vice presidential candidate Charles G. Dawes to speak to them at the Auditorium. A few long-distance calls and letters went out from Bob Church's office at 392 Beale, and the Dawes visit was cancelled.[365] Church was able to demonstrate his influence in the party on other occasions.

On July 10, 1925, federal judge William Ross was killed when his automobile ran off the highway near Jackson, Tennessee. He had just been indicted by the Madison County grand jury for larceny, fraudulent breach of trust and accessory to embezzlement, in proceedings following the collapse of the People's Savings Bank of Jackson.[366] There was feeling in Memphis that Ross had committed suicide. Since Republicans controlled the White House, even Crump conceded that a Democrat had little chance of being appointed to the judgeship to replace Ross.[367] While Memphis lawyers traveled to Washington to consult with Attorney General Sargent, Bob Church and Congressman J. Will Taylor met with President Coolidge at his summer retreat in Swampscott, Massachusetts.[368] Church is said to have favored Harry B. Anderson, who was indeed appointed by Coolidge on September 20, 1925.[369] Anderson, a Republican of course, was a respected attorney and son of one of the owners of the Anderson-

Bob Church Jr., in his office, the wall covered with photos of Republican presidents and other prominent Republicans. *Hooks Brothers.*

Tully Lumber Company of Memphis. He was endorsed by the local bar association as well.[370] Nevertheless, in the period between his appointment and his confirmation by the Senate, charges of leniency in enforcing the law, especially in Prohibition matters, led to hearings before the U.S. Senate Judiciary Committee.[371]

Church stood by Anderson,[372] and he was openly supported by *Commercial Appeal* editor C.P.J. Mooney and Senator Kenneth McKellar.[373] Crump also favored Anderson but avoided appearing on his behalf at the Senate hearings.[374] On January 29, 1926, Anderson was finally confirmed.[375] Crump attributed the opposition to Anderson to Klan elements.[376]

In the spring of 1926, the term of the incumbent Republican postmaster at Memphis, Saul Seches, was about to expire. The names of candidates for the expected replacement examination were bruited about, including H.C. McKellar, Democratic brother of Senator Kenneth McKellar and the assistant postmaster since 1918, when the Democrats held the White House.[377] Bob Church favored G. Tom Taylor (no kin to the Klansman) for the post[378] and opposed the rumored appointment of Seches without an examination.[379] Church's pressure on Washington was sufficient to ensure the holding of an examination, and he saw to it that Taylor was appointed even though he was over the civil service age limit.[380]

African American Memphians in the 1920s unobtrusively acted out their involuntary roles in the eyes of whites as town characters and second-class citizens. In Bob Church, they had a leader whose voice was at least heard, even in the White House. Ironically, however, it was not until the party that Church opposed came to power that a response more meaningful to the average Black citizen was received in Memphis.

CHAPTER 15

POLITICAL PORTENTS

O n October 2, 1925, E.H. Crump was fifty-one years old and the half owner of what was said to be the largest real estate mortgage loan business in the city of Memphis. To the resurgent rumors that his business would prevent him from being active in politics, he replied:

> *I am still carrying my card in the Ward Workers Band, which I joined about twenty years ago. I am not an aspirant for a place in the Gold Cornet Band, but no matter to what proportions my business grows, and it is growing fast, I still have time and always will have time to confer with the "boys" on matters political.*[381]

"Matters political" consisted of a hodgepodge of minor battles in which, as usual, Crump played no small role. In 1925, clashes still occurred between the county forces and the defeated Klansmen. In March, sheriff's deputies were accused of beating up Klan "Cyclops" Matt Grantham after he charged them with misdeeds. Klansmen felt constrained to place a guard around Grantham's home, although Sheriff Knight denied any misconduct on the part of his men.[382]

Shortly thereafter, according to "well-defined reports" printed in the *Commercial Appeal*, a council of war was held by Klan-supported "independents" of the last election. Among those present at the meeting at the Chisca Hotel were said to be the defeated candidate for sheriff, Will Taylor, Matt Grantham and Prohibition agent Joe Phillips. It was supposedly planned to "get" Sheriff Knight and chief Prohibition agent W.R. Wright by charging them with receiving payoffs from bootleggers. Knight would be ousted and Wright replaced by Phillips. It was said that some fifteen bootleggers were approached and offered immunity from federal prosecution if they would sign affidavits to the effect that they were buying "protection" from the sheriff's office and Prohibition authorities.[383] When rumors of the conspiracy were published, the alleged participants denied everything, and no more was heard of the matter.[384]

No more, that is, than a postscript written by E.H. Crump himself, both literally and figuratively. Believing Matt Grantham's attorney, Dave Puryear, to be the source of rumors and accusations against himself and his organization, Crump was not in the best frame of mind for an encounter with the gentleman. Writing to his friend Senator McKellar in July, Crump described the result of their meeting: "So, with my coat on my arm, I walked into the Tennessee Club barber shop [now the Burch, Porter & Johnson building on Court Square] and found Puryear there, also with his coat off. It all boiled out of me at the sight of him, and I exacted satisfaction before others interfered. That's all there is to it."[385]

The sinister "fee system" by which justices of the peace, through their deputies, arrested innocent Black people for the purpose of collecting fines and jail fees came to a head in 1925, when a deputy was convicted of shooting and killing an innocent Black woman in her moving car. The *Commercial Appeal*, incensed by the incident, demanded curtailment of the deputies' powers of arrest.[386] Crump also opposed the notorious practice.[387] For a while, the publicity seemed to restrain the justices, who left arrests to regular sheriff's deputies.[388] By October, however, the system was functioning again, and criminal court judge Richards accidentally discovered the practice of recruiting cotton pickers by paying their "fines" in return for their labor.[389] At the news of this virtual peonage, Sheriff Knight stepped in and ordered the deputy sheriffs attached to justices to serve only civil papers and refrain from wholesale arrests.[390] Despite the combined opposition of the newspapers, the sheriff and Crump, the fee system survived, and as late as 1927, reports persisted of its continuation. By then, helpless Chinese were also preyed upon.[391]

Crump met with more success when he decided to rid the county court of an opponent, Squire Finley, who had opposed Squire Gowen for chairman and supported Coroner Ingram in his ouster battle.[392] During the 1925 General Assembly (the state legislature), a private act sometimes referred to as a "ripper bill" was sponsored by the county forces. It redistricted Squire Finley quite out of office.[393]

The impending summer election of 1926 was to bring to an end the period of relative calm in city and county politics and lay the groundwork for elimination by Crump of another and more important political enemy. Austin Peay, an able Democrat, had been elected governor of Tennessee in 1922 over Crump's opposition. He was reelected in 1924 with Crump's tacit approval.[394] Crump had reasons for opposing Peay, who decided in 1926 to run for an almost unprecedented third term. Peay had been supported since his first gubernatorial race in 1918 by Luke Lea of Nashville. Lea, a wealthy businessman, was owner of the *Nashville Tennessean* newspaper at this time and a political power in middle Tennessee. He had gained some fame at the end of World War I, when he came close to kidnapping the ex-kaiser of Germany from his exile in the Netherlands. As far back as 1909, Lea had clashed with Crump when he opposed the Crump-supported bill that gave Memphis commission government.[395] Lea had also opposed Crump's good friend Kenneth McKellar ever since McKellar defeated Lea for the United States Senate in 1916.[396] Peay's control of the state election commission also meant appointment of hostile forces on the local election commission.[397]

No governor since the Civil War had been elected to a third term, and the continued control of state-appointed offices naturally carried the potential of building a self-perpetuating "machine." Crump was also believed to feel that the gasoline and tobacco taxes initiated by Peay had operated unfairly against the state's cities in favor of the rural areas.[398] The most important cause of his antipathy toward Peay, however, was the fact that Crump had chosen state treasurer Hill McAlister as his candidate for governor at least a year before.[399]

It has been said that the Democratic primary of 1926 marked the beginning of Crump's real interest in state politics.[400] Without doubt, Crump devoted much of his time and thought to the race and to his candidate, Hill McAlister. He believed that "the evolution question," raised so memorably by the Scopes trial the previous summer, would be a determining factor in the 1926 race. He lamented the fact that McAlister, who, according to Crump, "wrote" the Butler Act, had not spoken up at the time of the Scopes trial and thereby gained equal popularity with the voters as Peay, who had signed the anti-evolution bill into law.[401] When McAlister finally formally entered the race, Crump worried about his prospects. He wrote to Senator McKellar:

> *In my opinion Hill McAlister will have to do more than he has been doing to win. If in some way he could be made to realize the importance of*

Governor Austin Peay and his wife. *Author's collection.*

stirring up something to attract attention, it would be a wonderful help to his campaign. It may be that when he gets on the stump he will put some life into his race. Of course Peay is working in every way. He is giving, for example, insurance all over the state in large and small towns, including the state penitentiary buildings which were never insured before.[402]

There was to be a general election for county offices in August 1926. Crump brought out a ticket of candidates that was unopposed, except for Sheriff Knight, who was also backed by Mayor Paine. In May and June 1926, the Crump organization mounted an intensive drive to persuade Memphians to pay their poll taxes, and registration rose to an unusually high forty-four thousand.[403] Within thirty minutes of the announcement by Earl Barnard on July 17 as a candidate for sheriff against Will Knight, eight cars were hurrying about, bringing in voters for registration.[404]

But in the race for the gubernatorial nomination, tantamount to election, a fatal schism occurred. Mayor Paine, Commissioner Allen and the balance of the city organization supported Governor Peay, while Crump's county forces backed Hill McAlister. The city forces were confident that their vote strength would reduce the McAlister vote greatly, increasing Peay's chances of victory. Policemen and other city employees were set to work on the campaign. The county forces were equally confident that McAlister would get a majority of between ten thousand and twelve thousand votes in Shelby County.[405]

The campaign was heated, and Peay pictured himself as the champion of the people, fighting the urban bosses. In his final west Tennessee speech at Dyersburg, he stated defiantly that "Crump of Memphis can't beat me, [Mayor Hilary] Howse of Nashville and [Commissioner Edward] Bass of Chattanooga can't beat me."[406] The *Commercial Appeal*, Crump's traditional enemy, sided with Governor Peay. The *News Scimitar*, usually close to Crump but an opponent in 1924, enthusiastically supported McAlister, giving reasons that coincided with Crump's. In fact, the newspaper's editorial language began to sound very similar to Crump's own colorful style in his paid political advertisements. The "city machines," which the paper had found so distasteful in 1924, were now identified as "the voters of Memphis, Nashville and Knoxville." The *News Scimitar* was contemptuous of Paine's support of Peay as being worth only two votes: Paine's and his wife's. In a Crump-like vein, the paper added, "Paine's support of Peay is important only in that it shows what has been known a long time to many, that his sense of political gratitude is nil, and that he has been taking lessons in the gentle art of sucking eggs."[407]

Peay carried the state by a mere eight thousand votes in the August 5 primary.[408] The prediction by the county forces of the vote was accurate. The *Commercial Appeal* described election day under a headline that screamed, "Negroes Gang Polls for Hill McAlister in Rape of Ballots—Orgy of Debauchery Hits Bottom in Primary." The paper continued in a bitter tone:

> *In an orgy of Negro herding that paled old Rickwriting days into piping times of peace the machine smashed through for Hill McAlister yesterday in Shelby County with a majority of more than twelve thousand....The machine started early and kept at it late. This followed the juggling of primary officers to eliminate every city administration man suspected of any leanings for Peay. Then they started voting the Negroes. They voted them by the thousands. No literacy test was applied. It was not even necessary for the Negroes to mark their ballots. Registration certificates and poll tax receipts did not even count as scraps of paper.*

Car loads of the dusky-skinned McAlister Democrats made the polling places with clock-like regularity. Many of the cars were driven by white men; Negro women were voted just as deftly as the men. White men acted as their chauffeurs.

A vote a second was the ratio often during the day in the First Precinct of the Tenth Ward. They walked right in, they turned right around, and they walked right out again.

One of the Negroes was caught red handed voting twice in the Twelfth Ward....He was arrested by patrolmen....Commissioner Allen says he will stick to the case until the Negro is sent over the rocks.

The Negro said he was one of Harry Kinsky's Negroes. He said that gentleman gave him his poll tax receipt and his registration certificate. Inspector Griffin ordered Kinsky brought in, but when detectives went after him, they found that he was an election officer and they could not touch him without a warrant.[409]

The *Commercial Appeal's* editor, C.P.J. Mooney, was indignant: "We have come into a time when an election in Shelby County means nothing but the will of those who sit at the ballot boxes as judges and clerks, and they do not act on their free will, but on orders from the crowd that controls them."[410]

The day after the primary, the *Commercial Appeal* printed a photograph that showed several African Americans standing at what appeared to be a voting station. The caption on the photograph was, "McAlister Democrats in action during the primary."[411] The *News Scimitar* immediately branded the photograph and caption a "fake" and chided the *Commercial Appeal* for failing to discover the fraud when the photograph was submitted to it. The *News Scimitar* reported that the photograph had been identified by several local Republican officials as portraying Blacks voting in the *Republican* primary.[412] Nor was this the only comment the evening paper made on the Democratic primary. It took issue with "Old Reliable" on the matter of voting frauds: "Thursday's election, while bitterly fought in every city and county precinct, ended without any marked disturbances. In fact, considering the tense feeling, it was unusually quiet, and Shelby County cast its usual vote."[413]

Substantiating the paper's last remark to some extent is the fact that fewer than twenty thousand votes were cast in Shelby County in the Democratic primary election in 1926, as opposed to over twenty-five thousand in 1924.[414] The *News Scimitar* offered, as further evidence of the regularity of the vote, the text of a telegram, allegedly from *Commercial Appeal* editor Mooney to the pro-Peay *Nashville Tennessean*. The telegram was supposed to have been sent around noon on election day, after Mooney had toured all the larger city wards. The material parts of that text read:

> *So far only four or five Negroes offered to vote in the Democratic primary. It looks now as if the total vote of the city will not be over twelve thousand. There has been no disorder except in two small wards. The McAlister machine may attempt to rush in a vote later, but they will have a hard time finding voters.* [415]

The Democratic election officials discounted as "the usual wails of a losing side" the charge of illegal "herding" of African Americans to the polls in automobiles,[416] although it has been said by one writer that Bob Church helped procure a large turnout of Black voters.[417]

When the reports of alleged voting frauds appeared in other newspapers in the state, county forces feigned indignation and pointed out that every ward and district in Shelby County went overwhelmingly for McAlister. "The truth is," wrote Senator McKellar, "there were few Peay supporters in Shelby County. Peay had no organization. On the other hand McAlister had a splendid organization in both city and county."[418]

The results of the election recalled a joking letter that Crump had written to Senator McKellar earlier in the campaign. Crump had read one of McKellar's Prohibition speeches to his political lieutenant, Frank Rice, who had made a sour face. "Frank said he would like to know if your statement that drinking leads one to falsify, to steal, to be dishonest, and oftentimes to the commission of all kinds of crime, really covered stuffing the ballot box for a friend, or if that could be classed as a public welfare service."[419]

The *News Scimitar* analyzed the result of the Democratic primary:

> *If ever there was a politician repudiated, if ever a public officeholder was shown as a political nullity, it was Rowlett Paine on last Thursday.... With the Police Department under his control and openly trying in defiance of all civic decency to use it for political purposes; with city employees and their families ordered to fight under his banner, and with the strongest support the self-admitted "South's greatest snoozepaper"' was able to give, Paine gathered in for Peay the munificent sum of 3,687 votes.* [420]

The November 1926 general election was quiet, the Crump candidates for the legislature winning handily, although Peay was reelected governor. It seems probable that Crump told his supporters to stay home to see what

Clifford Davis, E.W. Hale, Walter Chandler, E.H. Crump, Will Gerber (*in rear*), K.D. McKellar, Watkins Overton and others in the 1930s. *Hooks Memphis Public Library.*

sort of turnout the city forces could muster. The light voting seemed to give him his answer.[421]

As the 1927 General Assembly was about to convene in Nashville, Crump felt that he should personally attend the session, although Frank "Roxy" Rice, his executive officer and right-hand man, was confident that he had things well in hand.[422] It was to be an important legislature for Governor Peay. Flushed with victory, he was to seek and obtain reenactment of the tobacco tax as a permanent revenue measure, and more highway and rural school funds were appropriated.[423] A leading light of Crump's legislative delegation was Watkins Overton, scion of a prominent Memphis family, a world war veteran and an attorney.[424] The real power over the delegation, however, was wielded by Frank Rice, who did not always take the representatives into his confidence.[425]

The legislature convened in early January 1927, and the Crump forces lost the initial battle when the speakership of the Senate (which is also the office of the lieutenant governor) went to Henry Horton, rather than to the Crump-approved candidate.[426] The alleged scandal of the August 1926

Democratic primary returned to haunt the Shelby County forces. The City Club of Memphis, backed by Peay forces and Memphis newspapers, sent a delegation, including Dave Puryear, to Nashville to demand an investigation of the primary. The anti-Crump forces at first planned to call a joint session of the General Assembly to request a resolution condemning the election frauds, but when their chances of success appeared doubtful, they called a mass meeting instead. The Shelby forces called a meeting of their own, which Crumpite Charles Bryan held spellbound.

The Nashville Tennessean, owned by Luke Lea, harped on the corruption theme, and there were rumors of a legislative investigation committee with a Crump foe, G.T. Fitzhugh, as counsel. The legislature was not prepared to air Shelby's dirty linen, however. Both houses passed resolutions expressing confidence in the Shelby delegation and denying the request of the City Club.[427]

"Peay's power with everything back of him is tremendous," wrote Overton to McKellar.[428] Despite this power, however, the Shelby forces and their allies were able to defeat Peay's attempts to pass a bill setting up an income tax and allowing farm property to be assessed for taxes at a lower rate than city property.[429] The county delegation also weathered Peay's onslaughts sufficiently to surprise themselves by electing the state treasurer.[430] Most important, the legislative session had given experience and publicity to some new faces in the Crump organization who would be heard from sooner than expected.

CHAPTER 16

THE FLOOD OF 1927

The 1927 legislature had hardly adjourned when a natural disaster shifted the interest and energies of Memphians from politics to more elemental problems. In 1927, an extraordinary coincidence of flood conditions in all the chief tributaries of the Mississippi River caused the most serious flooding by that river that had ever been recorded up to that time. Before it was over in June, an area of more than twenty-three thousand square miles had been flooded, and 700,000 people had been driven from their homes.[431]

Memphians eagerly scanned their newspapers for the "Flood News at a Glance." Levees were giving way, and towns were inundated in Missouri, Illinois, Kentucky, west Tennessee, Arkansas, Louisiana and Mississippi. Government engineers patrolled the levees from Cairo to New Orleans by land, river and air. Part of North Little Rock was under water, west Tennessee streams were flooding their banks and roads, such as the Jefferson Davis Highway to Dyersburg, were severed by water.[432]

By mid-April, the possibility of danger to Memphis and Shelby County alarmed the county commission, so that workhouse prisoners were put to work clearing undergrowth and placing sandbags at the south end of the south Memphis levee.[433] E.H. Crump himself came to inspect the levees.[434] Payne Avenue at Chelsea Street was under six inches of water,[435] and five county roads were closed.[436] By April 19, Memphis began to receive urgent appeals for aid from the surrounding countryside.[437] By April 21, Memphis was out of rail contact with St. Louis, Little Rock, Pine Bluff and

Prisoners sandbagging the levee during the flood. *Robert Ledbetter.*

the Southwest. The river stage at Memphis was forty-four and eight-tenths feet. For the first time since the flood of 1913, the Tri-State Fairgrounds were converted into a refugee camp for the flood victims. The Gene Lewis–Olga Worth theatrical company raised funds for the refugees with a benefit performance at the Loew's Palace theater.[438]

By train, boat, wagon, automobile and foot, the first five hundred refugees from the floodwaters arrived in Memphis on April 21. Memphians brought clothing and bedding to the Auditorium, where workers from the PTA sorted and repaired it. Refugees were tagged and assigned to tents at the Fairgrounds.[439] Local druggists donated medicine, and Bry's Department Store donated a pound of candy to each refugee child. Relief in the amount of $5 million ($80 million today) was raised nationally in response to President Coolidge's appeals, and by early May, Memphians had raised $93,000 ($1.25 million today) by themselves.[440] Today, the federal government would declare a disaster area and federal funds would flow in. The president would be expected to fly in and demonstrate that he "feels their pain." But not in 1927.

Shelby County was fortunate compared to its neighbors. No serious health problems arose because of the flood, as precautions against typhoid and similar diseases were carefully followed. By the end of April, all Shelby County roads were open.[441]

The African Americans in the Memphis refugee camps seem to have received equal (if separate) distribution of food, shelter and clothing,[442] although there were strong rumors that refugees from the plantations were watched by guards, sent by their landlords, to see that they returned to the plantation when waters subsided.[443]

In late April, Secretary of Commerce Herbert Hoover arrived in Memphis to assume control of flood relief work, and Memphis was made central rescue headquarters by him.[444] As in his work with Belgian relief in World War I, Hoover proved himself an able and efficient organizer. He traveled extensively throughout the flooded regions and reported on conditions to the nation over Memphis radio station WMC.[445] Soon, many southerners, forgetting their usual Democratic bias, began to remark that Hoover would make a fine president.[446] Most of the talk among civic leaders, however, was in the form of demands for congressional action to prevent a repetition of the disaster. A special session of Congress was urged to build a system of levees and spillways.[447] The *Commercial Appeal* asked, editorially: "Must not Congress now realize that piecemeal appropriations and disconnected work on methods of protection can never solve the problem…? If the Mississippi River is the Government's when it is an asset, it should also be the Government's when it is a liability."[448]

The great flood had temporarily turned Memphis's attention to its regional responsibilities. It was not long before local politics returned that attention to more parochial matters.

CHAPTER 17

CRUMP TAKES MEMPHIS

I n line with the vague promises of social and aesthetic programs in his second inaugural address in 1924, Mayor Paine envisioned great works to improve Memphis. Other southern cities took note when Paine put forth a $500 million plan to make Memphis a city beautiful and "wonder metropolis of the South." Mud Island was to be an amusement park, and the city was to be ringed by parks, with twenty acres of park for each square mile of city. The zoo would be improved and strict zoning rules enforced.[449] The ideas, of course, were embodied in the vision of city planner Harland Bartholomew and his famous study, which became the inspiration, if not the blueprint, for future city planning.[450]

Paine worked on keeping the tax rate stable, requesting that the city issue $2 million worth of bonds. He sought the additional money for projects considerably more prosaic than Bartholomew's. Water and sewerage facilities needed to be extended throughout the city, and bonds issued in 1896 needed to be retired.[451] The mayor and commissioners announced that the city civil service system, in perfunctory use since 1910, would be rigidly applied in most city jobs.[452] The new policy was unable to prevent the "release" of numbers of policemen in 1924 and 1925 when budget tightening demanded retrenchment. At one time, the police department was down to 278 men.[453]

Mayor Paine disproved rumors of his affiliation with local utility interests in 1925 when he traveled to Nashville to protest cuts by the state

Main Street, looking north from Union Avenue, 1927. *Memphis Heritage.*

board of equalization in the tax assessment valuation of the Memphis Power and Light Company and the Memphis Street Railway Company. Paine not only decried the loss of $35,000 in city revenue but also asked that assessments be raised.[454] City affairs under Mayor Paine, "peculiarly free of politics," as the *Commercial Appeal* had remarked, were managed with little excitement. The mayor would address a Sunday Bible class and preside at the launching of some new passenger train, while fire and police commissioner Thomas Allen would, typically, plan a crusade against jaywalking.[455] Things were not as tranquil in relations between the city and county political organizations. In spite of the relatively unblemished record of the Paine administration, a fierce and bitter struggle awaited Paine's attempt to win a third term as mayor.

The tenuous four-year alliance between Paine and Crump forces had been destroyed in the heat of the summer campaigns of 1926. By the spring of 1927, Crump had already decided to regain control of city affairs. At best, the alliance with Paine had only been a marriage of convenience, and Crump had never been a Paine enthusiast. It only remained for him to organize the campaign and announce his slate of candidates.[456]

Crump's first step was to gain control of the county election commission, which controlled the county's election machinery. Not only was a city election at stake, but Crump's friend and ally Kenneth McKellar was running for reelection to the U.S. Senate. The state election commission, composed of a Peay Democrat, a Crump Democrat and a Republican, was in charge of appointing the county election commissioners. Crump's lieutenant, Frank Rice, traveled to Nashville in late May 1927 and sat in on the meeting of the state commissioners. With him he carried a list of Crump-McKellar men that the Crump commissioner dutifully followed in making his appointments for each county. John Brown, a leading Crumpite in the recent legislature, was chosen as one of the Shelby County Democratic commissioners. The Peay commissioner named Crump's enemy, Galen Tate, as the other Shelby Democrat. Control of the county commission now hinged on the Republican member.[457] The Republicans hesitated for almost a month, and rumor had it that Bob Church was reluctantly consulted by the county forces.[458] On July 26, the suspense ended. Ross A. Mathews, a former law associate of Senator McKellar, was appointed over the complaint of the "Lily-Whites" that he was not really a Republican.[459] Mathews immediately voted to elect John Brown chairman of the commission.[460]

The Bellomini scandal, involving charges of payoffs to police and sheriff's deputies by a bootlegger, broke into the news in the spring of 1927. The matter took on political overtones when Mayor Paine asked federal, rather than county, officials to investigate. District state attorney general Tyler McLain, a Crump acolyte, called the procedure "asinine."[461] Paine responded that McLain did not want an investigation and that his comment was "a feeble echo of his master's voice...and disclosed plainly

Left to right: Charles Bryan, Joe Boyle, E.H. Crump and Frank Rice at a party for children. *Hooks Memphis Public Library*.

the purpose of his actions." For the first time, Paine began to speak of "gang politics." He warmed to his subject: "When I urged a federal grand jury investigation I struck deeper than I thought!...McLain showed the kind of investigation he makes when last year he probed the Democratic Primary and found nothing wrong."[462]

The *Commercial Appeal* joined the attack with a fierce editorial that called McLain "Fatty" and charged that "his not too acute" nostrils missed the "stench" of the August primary.[463] The opening guns of the city election campaign of 1927 had been fired, although neither side had put forth a ticket yet.

By mid-summer, speculation was rampant. Black citizens were publicly organizing to vote, but their choice was not then known. City commissioner Thomas Allen announced his intention to quit when his term expired. City judge Clifford Davis would only say that he would not run for judge again. Mayor Paine was noncommittal.[464] The Crump forces were busy behind the scenes, wooing Judge Davis and planning to "get Paine." Watkins Overton was considered a likely candidate for Crump's ticket, being "tried and trusted" and being one of those "who knew their places." It was rumored that Crump forces would be cautious in the election, due to Galen Tate's access to the voter roll books and the statewide attention drawn by the infamous primary election of the preceding year.[465]

The Crump forces were successful in wooing Davis. He spurned Paine's overtures, remembering his dismissal as Paine's secretary several years before.[466] After a conference between Davis and Overton at Davis's office, the Crump ticket for city commission was finally announced on August 20. Watkins Overton would seek the office of mayor, his friends pointing to his "progressive, liberal," pro-labor record in the legislature. Clifford Davis was their candidate for vice mayor and police commissioner. A Mississippian, Davis had lived in Memphis for sixteen years as an attorney, Paine's secretary and city judge. Sam M. Jackson, a Spanish-American War veteran and business manager of the YMCA, sought a commission job. O.I. Kruger, a leather worker's union officer and businessman, was put forward to please the labor vote. A.P. "Tony" Walsh, connected with cotton and banking interests, was expected to help capture the business vote.

Significantly, Frank Rice was charged with announcing the platform. Lower and more stable taxes were promised as "high point no. 1." Tweaking Paine's nose, the ticket also pledged:

1. A lower death rate
2. A lower murder rate
3. Fewer bonds
4. Attention to city business
5. Economy
6. No secret payrolls
7. Impartiality in street work
8. More small parks
9. Honest police without sensational "drives"
10. New industry[467]

If many of these promises seem esoteric, apparently they meant something to the Memphians of the day. A Watkins Overton Veterans Club was founded, chaired by attorney and veteran Walter Chandler, to attract the votes of young World War I veterans.

No word came from Paine, though his friends urged him to act quickly.[468] On August 30, while standing on the corner of Adams and Second Streets

Above: E.H. Crump followed by Watkins Overton and Samuel Bates. *University of Memphis Special Collections.*

Left: Cliff Davis peeks over Crump's shoulder. *Hooks Memphis Public Library.*

talking to a newsman, Paine was approached by E.H. Crump and Dave Wells. The following conversation was reported:

Crump: "Hello, Mr. Mayor."

Paine: "How are you, Mr. Crump?"

Crump: "Why don't you go on and get out your ticket? We're going to beat you sure."

Paine: "What are you campaigning around the courthouse for? You ought to go out in the city where the votes are."

Crump: "We're getting them to pay their poll taxes, you know. They have to come up here to get their receipts."

Paine: Oh, I don't know about that. They tell me they're paying them out in the city."

The men laughed, joked a bit more and parted.[469]

At the beginning of the race, Paine was confident of victory.[470] The day after his sidewalk encounter with Crump, Paine announced his candidacy and the names of his running mates. He still had no political headquarters and virtually no organization or platform. He merely stated his opposition to "Boss Rule" and "government by proxy" from "the private office of a political boss." His ticket consisted of himself; Mrs. Edgar Lee, a clubwoman and member of the PTA; C.A. Price, district manager of a foundry; and Ceylon Blackwell, a world war veteran and engineer in the tradition of Thomas H. Allen. Incumbent commissioner of public utilities, roads and bridges Horace Johnson was also on the list. After the announcement, Paine went into a strategy meeting in his courthouse office with Allen, Galen Tate and others.[471] On September 8, Paine opened his campaign in earnest, and the theme was still independence from Crump. Before an audience of two hundred, mostly city employees, Paine promised that "the day of ballot box stuffing and election thievery is over in Memphis."[472]

Both sides were now actively seeking voters. Under the law, there was no permanent registration. Would-be voters were required to register every two years and pay a poll tax of $2.10 before they could vote. The last registration had been in August 1927, and another would be held ten days before the election.[473] Galen Tate, the anti-Crump election commissioner, charged that ten thousand fraudulent registration certificates had been issued in the August registration.[474]

Paine continued on the offense, charging that his administration had been burdened with paying off all of the bonds issued during Crump's terms as mayor. Overton promised to allow city taxes to be paid in four installments instead of all at once. Paine countered by charging that this was merely a scheme to enrich Crump's henchman, Frank Rice, who was collector of back taxes and penalties thereon. To Overton's pledge of biennial tax assessments, he replied that this would give the rich a year of tax-free improvements. He also pointed to the fact that the county's assessments were 10 percent higher than the city's.[475]

In late September, Paine finally came out with a platform. He pledged:

1. Low, equal taxes
2. Honest elections
3. Fair city-county school fund split
4. A municipal airport
5. More swimming pools
6. Municipal band concerts
7. More parks
8. Extended street rail lines
9. Fire prevention
10. Higher pay for police
11. Just treatment of "Negroes"
12. Suburban railroad stations[476]

On September 21, Paine opened his headquarters. The strenuous handshaking phase of the campaign had not yet begun.[477] Paine workers were preparing for the November election, however. In many of the city's wards and precincts, there were no Paine supporters to serve as election officers and thereby help supervise the voting. This deficiency was remedied by having Paine men move into the ward or precinct twenty days before the election, thereby becoming eligible for appointment.[478]

Overton headquarters opened on October 4, and campaign manager Walter Chandler, president of the Tennessee Bar Association, announced that the county forces had already organized every ward and precinct in the city.[479] Organizational matters proceeded in both camps through most of October. Overton's headquarters put out campaign buttons with the likenesses of Overton and Davis, with "Lower Taxes" written above the images and "Easy Payments" below. Voters in each ward were being carefully checked.[480]

Charges were exchanged through the newspapers. Paine recalled Crump's ouster in 1915 for failure to enforce the laws against alcohol and charged

Union Avenue looking west, with a Paine campaign sign on the Tennessee Hotel, 1927. *Hooks Memphis Public Library.*

that Crump hoped to suppress investigation of the Bellomini scandal. He compared the city's 72 percent raise in tax assessments in the period from 1919 to 1926 to the county's 142 percent raise.[481] Crump defended the fiscal policies of his administrations and dubbed the mayor "Mr. High Tax Paine."[482] Paine called Overton a "young lad" and lashed out at the county government for unfairly dividing school funds so that the county could reduce its taxes by two cents, while the city had to use hospital-intended money from its general fund to make up the school deficit.[483]

In late October, election commissioner John Brown charged Paine with sending forty policemen to supplemental registration booths to solicit for him. Paine admitted that the police were there but stated that they were sent to prevent repetition of the alleged frauds of the August primary. He announced that a partial check of the August voter registration "shows a widespread conspiracy to violate the election laws. Hundreds and hundreds of Negroes were registered illegally in the August registration to offset the votes of decent, self-respecting white people."[484] A citizens committee, formed to check on registration frauds, checked on 2,000 names and found 224 to be fraudulent or improper. Some were dead or moved, and some listed vacant lots as addresses. The committee pointed a finger at neither side, but Overton manager Walter Chandler promised to produce some of the "dead" voters.[485]

The final, formal opening of the campaign came on October 24 at Gaston Park in south Memphis. The autumn night was clear and balmy as a well-attended Paine rally was opened by fireworks and a brass band. As the noise died down, Reverend J. Ralph Roberts made an unscheduled speech attacking New York governor Al Smith and Tammany Hall (1928 was a presidential election year, and Smith was a Democratic contender). Reverend Roberts was heckled by the audience, as was L.E. Gwinn, who attacked Cliff Davis and Tony Walsh. Paine diplomatically avoided comment on national politics. He pointed with pride to his administration and characterized Overton as an unknown.[486]

The next night at the same park, the Overton-Davis opening rally was held. Overton charged Paine with waste and fiscal irresponsibility. Jake Cohen, president of the trades and labor council, announced that 90 percent of labor was for Overton. Davis was introduced with his theme song, "Our Boy Cliff."[487]

Charges continued to fly, and soon the parties resorted to ridicule. Paine termed the Overton-Davis team a "minstrel show" because supporters rode to rallies in county school buses.[488] Davis retaliated by mimicking Paine publicly.[489] Smarting under Paine's continuous charges that Overton was his puppet, Crump purchased full-page advertisements in the papers. He denied that he sought any political office in person or by proxy, stating that his business claimed all of his time. "Further, I state that Watkins Overton will be the absolute Mayor of Memphis without dictation or embarrassment from me."[490]

Perhaps because of fear of Crump's successful control of Black votes, or because of desperation, Paine injected the race issue into the campaign. A Black organization, the West Tennessee Civic and Political League, registered thousands of Black Memphians to vote early in the campaign. The movement seems to have opposed Paine from the beginning but also sought to better their lot through bargaining with their voting strength. Their manifesto requested Black policemen in Black wards, access to the zoo and parks, better treatment by the police and higher teacher pay. Bob Church was apparently a prime mover in the organization, which claimed to control 40 percent of the registered Black voters. Church lieutenant George W.

Lee has said that Paine sought the group's support but was rebuffed. Many local African American leaders apparently felt that Paine had betrayed their support in the 1923 election and broken solemn promises to them. A city incinerating plant had been erected during his second term near a better Black residential and school area, causing much resentment.[491] Crump, sensing a good political issue, capitalized on the resentment and saw to it that the incinerator was blamed throughout the campaign on Paine.[492]

Paine's reaction to the Black group appeared immediately. He called them and their solidarity "the greatest menace to white supremacy in this city since reconstruction days."[493] He charged them with seeking to dominate city politics and promised that there would be no Black firemen or policemen and no removal of the park restrictions as long as he had a say in the matter. Overton had no immediate comment on Paine's statement, although another Crump advertisement on the same day confidently claimed 99.10 percent of Black votes for Overton.[494]

The next day, Overton issued a carefully constructed comment on Paine's remarks. They had, after all, not been an attack on his ticket. Overton reminded voters that Paine had accepted the support of the Black group's predecessor in 1923 and chided the mayor for raising the race issue:

> *No mayor* [said Overton] *since the Civil War has ever questioned white supremacy and none has ever run upon a platform seeking to defend it.... Thou hypocrite: first cast the beam out of thine own eye....Is there any difference between...1923 and now, except that by oppression and broken promises, and the building of an obnoxious city crematory in the choicest Negro residential district of the city and within a stone's throw of their most prominent schools Paine has hopelessly lost the thinking Negro voter....We do not favor anything which might create race friction. Therefore we are opposed to Negro police, Negro firemen and general admission to the white parks.*[495]

Overton did promise, however, to seek more Black parks, pools and hospital facilities, realizing that "the general improvement of the Negroes as citizens is part of the general plan for the improvement of the South."[496] On the defensive, Paine denied any deals with Blacks in the 1923 election and sarcastically suggested that "if Mr. Overton is custodian of the records kept by any Negro club, I shall welcome his publication of any statement I may have made."[497]

At a sparsely attended meeting of the Black group in the Beale Avenue Baptist Church on Halloween, the question of whether to endorse a ticket was debated. Some feared future consequences of an endorsement, and others balked at approving ex-Klansman Clifford Davis. But league secretary M.S. Stewart noted that Paine's remarks had made the choice for them and that Overton had promised many of their goals without solicitation. The Overton ticket was endorsed.[498]

Paine responded with the charge that a deal had been made between Crump forces and Bob Church in return for overlooking $22,000 in back taxes owed by Church. Overton denied any deal and promised to treat Blacks "just as all true Southern gentlemen think they should be treated."[499] There had been no need for a "deal." The choice had been relatively easy for the African Americans.[500]

As election day drew near, an incident occurred that spotlighted tensions generated by Paine's fear of a repetition of the alleged voting irregularities in the August 1926 primary. In late summer, a Black gas station worker, Julius Grayson, was partaking of a warm afternoon's relaxation with his neighbors on his street. A large car pulled to the curb, driven by a white man who identified himself as F.W. Burgoyne. Burgoyne inquired of the "boys" whether they were registered to vote. When they replied that they were not, he offered to drive them to the registration booth. Their protestations of inability to pay the poll tax were silenced by Burgoyne's assurance that all that "would be taken care of." The registration went smoothly, and the newly enfranchised Blacks were deposited at their front doors once again. Before leaving, however, Burgoyne collected their registration papers, which he promised to "attend to." Julius Grayson and his friends were not sure how the papers had been "attended to" until early November, when Grayson observed a white grocer in their neighborhood going through a stack of registration papers in his store. He was heard to remark that Julius's papers had no poll tax receipt with them.

Grayson had the sagacity to report the matter to his boss, who called the police. Assistant Chief John Plaxco, with Captain Tom Couch and Charles Rutland, rushed to the grocery on South Parkway to investigate. Checking a suspicious cracker box on a shelf, they found Julius's papers with others, with a poll tax receipt attached. Affixed to the stack was also an Overton-Davis "guidance card." Chief Plaxco turned the papers over to Galen Tate, asking that they be returned to the rightful owners, if valid. The next day, Plaxco claimed, he received a call from a former police official and Crump supporter who warned him to give up the papers or be arrested. When Plaxco demurred, one R.C. Craigo claimed to own one of the receipts and swore out a warrant for Plaxco's arrest. The arrest occurred at Paine's headquarters at Main and Madison, where Deputy Sheriff Garibaldi found Plaxco and marched him off to jail. Plaxco cooled his heels for two hours until bond could be made. He was charged with larceny and receiving stolen property.[501]

The Crump forces regarded Chief Plaxco's arrest as a salutary example to forestall any officious meddling by police in the election.[502] Publicly, Crump forces put out the word that the grocer was only caring for the registration papers. Sheriff Knight feigned indignation at Plaxco's raid on the grocery without a warrant and vowed to arrest any other police acting illegally.[503] The city police commissioner retorted that the whole power of the police force would be used to see that the "legitimate" voter was given an honest election.[504]

By this time, the Citizens Committee of the City Club claimed to have found 759 of 900 registrations to be fraudulent.[505] Mayor Paine met with several friends and supporters and discussed the possibility of calling for National Guard troops to police the election against voting frauds. The idea was finally dropped, however, as Paine felt the move might hurt more than help.[506]

The *Commercial Appeal*, after reflecting on the campaign (and now free of the late Mooney's guiding hand and under new ownership), was surprisingly unconcerned with the controversy. It editorialized:

> *The partisans on both sides have so far deported themselves fairly well, all things considered....It is a mistake for anyone to think that the fate of Memphis is in the balance....Memphis will continue to grow and prosper, no matter who is elected....* [Vote], *go your way, and be sportsman enough to abide by the result. Keep cool, and probably three months hence you will have forgotten all about it.*[507]

Apparently considering themselves stalemated, the Police Department and Sheriff's Department signed an agreement to police the polls in harmony. Commissioner Allen instructed his men to stay impartial—and out of voting booths.[508]

The *Evening Appeal*, a new offshoot of the *Commercial Appeal*, had proposed steps to safeguard the honesty of the election. Paine adopted them and challenged Overton to accept them. Overton quickly accepted the proposals, which included dividing election officers equally between the rival tickets, allowing immediate checks on suspected voting irregularities and allowing each side an equal number of poll watchers in each precinct.[509]

The arrangement served to substantially increase the number of Paine's voting officers.[510]

Election day, November 10, came and went with surprising calm. To be sure, two Paine election officers were arrested by deputies for challenging Black voters too sharply, and police arrested one Black man for voting twice. But the expected flood of African American voters failed to materialize. In one precinct, Crump supporter Will Gerber teased a Paine man by pretending to suspect that his had not been "an honest box." The Paine supporter retorted that if Gerber did not think so, he should "come down off that stand." Gerber jumped down and punched the man in the face before he was dragged from the room by his friends.[511] In another precinct, a Paine supporter, a doctor, held the ballot box between his knees, hoping to thereby prevent any fraud. When the votes were finally counted and Paine received only one, the doctor admitted that his precinct's vote had been "painfully honest."[512]

The story was much the same throughout the city, as seventy-two of the city's seventy-four precincts went for the Overton-Davis ticket. Paine himself received a mere 6,948 votes to Overton's 19,548, and Clifford Davis led the other Crump commissioners with 20,978 votes. The only Crump candidate to lose was Phil Wallace, who was defeated by Davis's predecessor as city judge, L.T. Fitzhugh. The election was a stunning victory for Crump.[513]

As the outcome became clear early that night, E.H. Crump happily led a parade of winners from the big courthouse across the street to the neoclassic police station, where he encountered commissioner Thomas Allen.

"Well," said Allen, "you beat us."

"Well," said Crump, "I helped you twice."[514]

The *Commercial Appeal* reported the festivities that followed:

> *Ed Crump, Watkins Overton and Clifford Davis "took over" Memphis last night to the tune of "There'll Be a Hot Time in the Old Town Tonight." His face wreathed in the smile triumphant, the veteran campaigner, a hand on the arm of his proteges, the new mayor and vice mayor of Memphis, led a parade of their followers through downtown sections of Memphis. At their head most of the suspended members of the police department, the crowd swarmed into the Police Station where Messrs. Crump, Davis and Overton were getting the last returns of their overwhelming victory. There were shouts of "Hurrah for Crump!" and many for the victorious candidates, the noise reaching into the Commissioners' office where Mayor Paine and his loyal little group had spent the evening viewing the returns.*

The two elected candidates evaded their admirers long enough to dash off short statements for the public. Mr. Crump merely said: "The people have made their statement."

Out into the shouting, milling happy crowd, they went and the parade was formed, the band striking up the "Hot Time in the Old Town Tonight" song and "Hail, Hail, the Gang's All Here."

Cars were stopped in their tracks as the parade continued, gaining new marchers as they wended their way to Court Square. Here the parade stopped and the band struck up a lively air.[515]

They then proceeded, Overton and Davis being hoisted to the shoulders of their supporters. The crowd grew thicker, and finally even Crump was elevated, being carried into the elegant confines of the new Hotel Peabody lobby on the shoulders of several huskies. Leaving the Peabody, the parade made its way down Beale Street, where the "dusky citizenry" joined in the general acclaim. Completing its tour of the downtown area, the parade disbanded at Overton-Davis headquarters at 83 Madison, with shouts of victory. Smaller parades formed and continued. A group of suspended policemen came into police headquarters with a band, being greeted by the shout, "It won't be long now!" from many of their old comrades. The *Commercial Appeal* concluded the story:

Finally the tumult and the shouting simmered down to stray groups here and there about the city. The police station became unusually quiet. Someone said: "here comes the Mayor." And Mayor Paine came. If the result had been a disappointment, the mayor showed his gameness. He waved his hand at the boys about him. His magnificent little wife was by his side, as she had been…throughout…his campaign. The little group, composed of Mr. and Mrs. Paine, Senator L.E. Gwinn, John L. Exby, and others, walked out the rear of the [police] station and went into the night.[516]

CHAPTER 18

POST MORTEM

The era of independent city government, the Paine era, spawned by the public's contempt for professional politicians, was over. Amateurs in office had proved no equal to the redheaded professional without portfolio. The *Commercial Appeal* evaluated the 1927 election with insight, objectivity and charity:

> *Behind Overton was a perfect organization. Overton's strength came from those who would have supported any candidate that had the endorsement of the machine. To those who voted for Overton without knowing him and for no reason other than he was picked by the organization, we can give assurance that they voted wiser than they knew. Those who voted for him as a henchman did not know their man....Watkins Overton is worthy of the tradition of his name....Overton goes into office at a fortunate time for himself. The town is growing. Business is good. The people are contented and reasonably prosperous. There are no divisions and dissensions to consume his time. His energies may be devoted safely to the business of building a bigger and better Memphis.*
>
> *Mayor Paine will go out of office with the gratitude of the people for having given the city eight years of intelligent and progressive service. He was drafted for mayor when municipal politics was at its lowest ebb. Politics had made Memphis a joke and a by-word throughout the country. He redeemed the city and restored its name....Mayor Paine built the Auditorium, forced agreement for the construction of the Harahan Viaduct, compelled the*

railroads to reach agreements for the construction of viaducts within the city, and in scores of ways contributed to the development and progress of the city.…Had he been more concerned with politics he would have known that the city government was honeycombed with political disloyalty. He might have ferreted out the disloyalty and built a political organization of his own, but he was too busy doing bigger things.[517]

Before his victory parade through the streets on election night, Ed Crump had donned a new hat and suit, as if he realized that he was beginning a new role. He was now master of the county's government in totality. The final rung had been climbed on the ladder that was bottomed on the saloon alliances and strong-arm electioneering of early days. Unlike boss Frank Hague of New Jersey and James Curley of Boston, Crump, described by Jennings Perry as "this semi-literate old fellow with the steamed-apricot face and amazing hairy eyebrows,"[518] no longer needed the more primitive props of power. As so many times in his life, Crump spoke now of withdrawing from politics. In December 1927, he wrote to his friend Senator McKellar: "It is my purpose to help the boys out next August, and then to stand back and let others bear the heat and burden of the battle, for I have served my time."[519]

He really did not mean it. For another twenty-seven years, he would rule all of Shelby County, and Memphis would pass through more prosperous times, depressions and floods. The city would continue to grow in its own way, slowly and quietly, under the firm, familiar hand of Crump, until World War II would change the world forever.

Memphis after 1927 had a few more years to savor the Roaring Twenties. As though to symbolize the precarious balance of the decade and its zany prosperity, Alvin "Shipwreck" Kelly came to Memphis in 1928 to perform his peculiar but famous stunt of flagpole sitting. The site picked for his Memphis escapade was the Commercial Appeal building, then on Second Street at Court Square. He elevated himself to the flagpole, where he swayed in the breeze for considerable time, some 125 feet above Second and Court Streets. Great crowds of Memphians came to watch even after the illuminated *Commercial Appeal* baseball scoreboard blinked out for the night. Kelly quietly munched a sandwich and waved to the citizens below. Then, as evening came on, the crowds melted away, leaving the man to his thoughts.[520]

NOTES

Preface

1. Abels, *In the Time of Silent Cal*, 9–47; White, *Puritan in Babylon*, 260 *et seq.*
2. Coppock, *Memphis Sketches*, 7, 13; *Book of Three States*, 7, 13; Baker, *Memphis Commercial Appeal*, 269; *Commercial Appeal*, November 18, 1927, 1.
3. Miller, *Mr. Crump of Memphis*, 119; Bridges, "Editor Mooney vs. Boss Crump," *West Tennessee Historical Society Papers* 20 (1966): 101.
4. Kitchens, "Ouster of Mayor Edward H. Crump," 112.
5. *News Scimitar*, June 9, 1919, 7.
6. *Commercial Appeal*, June 9, 1919, 1.
7. Ibid., November 18, 1922, 3, 6; *News Scimitar*, November 18, 1922, 1.
8. House, *Cub Reporter*.
9. Stanton, "Blocked Editorials of C.P.J. Mooney," vol. 5, April 18, 1923.
10. Ibid., March 29, 1923.
11. Silver, "C.P.J. Mooney of the Commercial," 82; *Commercial Appeal*, August 1, 1926, February 28, 1926, 6.
12. Mooney, *Mid-South and Its Builders*, 702; *News Scimitar*, October 9, 1922, 1.
13. *Commercial Appeal*, February 4, 1922, 6.
14. Stanton, "Blocked Editorials of C.P.J. Mooney," vol. 7, March 18, 1923.
15. Tilly, "Memphis and the Mississippi Valley Flood," 43.
16. Blankenship, "*Commercial Appeal*'s Attack on the Ku Klux Klan," 51, 55.
17. Silver, "C.P.J. Mooney of *The Commercial Appeal*," 81, 82; Bridges, "Editor Mooney vs. Boss Crump," 79.

18. House, *Cub Reporter*, 126, 127.

19. Ibid., 136.

20. Geraghty, "Life and Editorials of C.P.J. Mooney," 103.

21. Silver, "C.P.J. Mooney of *The Commercial Appeal*," 82; Stanton, "Blocked Editorials of C.P.J. Mooney," vol. 11, July 29, 1923, 6.

22. Stanton, "Blocked Editorials of C.P.J. Mooney," vol. 5, May 27, 1923, 4.

23. *Commercial Appeal*, December 18, 1921, 6.

24. Ibid., January 8, 1922, 1.

25. Ibid., July 23, 1927, 1.

26. Young, *Standard History of Memphis*, 457; Stanton, "Blocked Editorials of C.P.J. Mooney," March 18, 1923.

27. *Commercial Appeal*, July 19, 1927, 1.

28. Miller, *Memphis during the Progressive Era*, 192–94.

29. Watson, "Memphis Sound," 25, 78 *et seq.*

30. Ibid., 84–86.

31. Stanton, "Blocked Editorials of C.P.J. Mooney," vol. 5, May 8, 1923.

32. *Commercial Appeal*, September 6, 1921, 6.

33. Ibid., October 13, 1921, 6.

34. Ibid., October 27, 1921, 6.

35. *Book of Three States*, 11.

36. Bridges, "Editor Mooney vs. Boss Crump," 82.

37. Stanton, "Blocked Editorials of C.P.J. Mooney," vol. 5, April 15, 1923.

38. Bridges, "Editor Mooney vs. Boss Crump," *passim*; McFerrin, *Caldwell and Company*, 88.

Chapter 1

39. Mowry, *Urban Nation*, 1.

40. May, *End of American Innocence*; Allen, *Only Yesterday*, 11 *et seq.*, 118.

41. Mowry, *Urban Nation*, x.

42. Ibid., 34.

43. Ibid., 36; Cash, *Mind of the South*, 263.

44. Allen, *Only Yesterday*, 112.

45. Mowry, *Urban Nation*, 8; Cash, *Mind of the South*, 265–72.

46. Cash, *Mind of the South*, 183 *et seq.*, 273.

47. Miller, *Memphis during the Progressive Era*, 3, 13, *et seq.*

Chapter 2

48. *Commercial Appeal*, January 1, 1924, 1; Allen, *Only Yesterday*, 112.

49. Cash, *Mind of the South*, 265.

50. Ibid.

51. Simkins, *South Old and New*, 375.

52. *Commercial Appeal*, July 19, 1924, 11; May 25, 1924, 21; September 26, 1927, 11.

53. Cossett Library, Memphis Tennessee, *Papers of Kenneth D. McKellar*, Watkins Overton to Kenneth D. McKellar, January 24, 1924.

54. *Commercial Appeal*, December 31, 1925, 9.

55. Ibid.

56. Cash, *Mind of the South*, 265.

57. *Commercial Appeal*, January 3, 1926, 6.

58. Ibid., September 15, 1927, 13.

59. Cash, *Mind of the South*, 265; White, *Puritan in Babylon*, 390.

60. Cash, *Mind of the South*, 268.

61. *Commercial Appeal*, January 13, 1924, 20; August 3, 1924, 12.

62. Ibid., September 2, 1925, 1; September 24, 1925, 12.

63. Ibid., October 18, 1924, 1; October 21, 1924, 1.

64. Allen, *Only Yesterday*, 114; *Commercial Appeal*, January 16, 1924, 1; Lynd and Lynd, *Middletown*, 253n.

65. *Commercial Appeal*, January 16, 1924, 1.

66. McIlwaine, *Memphis Down in Dixie*, 24.

67. *Commercial Appeal*, February 19, 1924, 11.

68. Ibid., May 31, 1925, 13; November 8, 1925, 16. The city limits were just east of the Fairgrounds in 1925.

69. *Commercial Appeal*, June 24, 1924, 1; June 27, 1924, 21; September 28, 1925, 8.

70. Ibid., March 1, 1924, 12.

71. Ibid., March 9, 1924, section V, 2.

72. Ibid., February 29, 1924, 13.

73. Ibid., January 13, 1924, 19.

74. Ibid., January 12, 1924, 7; January 13, 1924, 21; January 14, 1924, 3.

75. Ibid., December 31, 1924, 9.

76. Ibid., October 2, 1927, 1; May 14–16, 1927, 1.

77. Ibid., May 31, 1925, 1; January 19, 1924, 11; Allen, *Only Yesterday*, 54.

78. *Commercial Appeal*, January 10, 1924, 1.

79. Ibid., January 19, 1924, 6.

80. Ibid., January 1, 1926, 11; January 3, 1926, 11.
81. Ibid., January 10, 1924, 8.
82. Ibid., June 21, 1924, 4.
83. Ibid., June 28, 1924, 13.
84. Ibid., January 21, 1924, 3.
85. Ibid., February 16, 1926, 1; October 23, 1925, 1.
86. Ibid., June 7, 1925, 3.
87. Cash, *Mind of the South*, 265–73 *et seq.*; Allen, *Only Yesterday*, 121–28.
88. Tindall, "Business Progressivism," 101.
89. Grantham, *Democratic South*, 63.
90. Simkins, *South Old and New*, 288–89.
91. *Commercial Appeal*, January 10, 1924, 17.
92. *Papers of Kenneth D. McKellar*, Riechman to McKellar, April 8, 1924.
93. *Commercial Appeal*, February 28, 1926, 6.

Chapter 3

94. Miller, *Memphis during the Progressive Era*, 116–19; Miller, *Mr. Crump of Memphis*, 84, 85.
95. Phillips, "Rowlett Paine," 101.
96. *Commercial Appeal*, January 19, 1924, 11.
97. Ibid., January 20, 1924, 6.
98. Ibid., January 17, 1924, 11; April 5, 1925, 1.
99. Ibid., January 16, 1924, 6.
100. Ibid., January 6, 1924, 6.
101. Ibid., February 16, 1924, 6.
102. Ibid., January 1, 1924, 16; January 4, 1924, 9; January 13, 1924, 15.
103. McIlwaine, *Memphis Down in Dixie*, 24.
104. Folmsbee, Corlew and Mitchell, *History of Tennessee*, 381.
105. *Commercial Appeal*, January 5, 1964, section V, 1.
106. Ibid., August 1, 1925, 12.
107. Ibid., February 28, 1924, 24.

Chapter 4

108. Ibid., July 6, 1927, 5.
109. Ibid., August 25, 1925, 10.

110. Ibid., February 6, 1924, 6.
111. Ibid., December 17, 1925, 12.
112. Cash, *Mind of the South*, 266.
113. Allen, *Only Yesterday*, 113.
114. Cash, *Mind of the South*, 263.
115. *Commercial Appeal*, December 7, 1925.
116. Vance, *Human Factors in Cotton Culture*, 144–46.
117. *Commercial Appeal*, February 8, 1924, 11.

Chapter 5

118. Miller, *Memphis during the Progressive Era*, 148–56.
119. Miller, *Mr. Crump of Memphis*, 77–116; Bridges, "Editor Mooney vs. Boss Crump," 77–107.
120. Bridges, "Editor Mooney vs. Boss Crump," 117–28.
121. Phillips, "Rowlett Paine, Mayor of Memphis," 96, 97.
122. Miller, *Mr. Crump of Memphis*, 130.
123. *Commercial Appeal*, August 5, 1924, 6.
124. Phillips, "Rowlett Paine, Mayor of Memphis," 104, 105.
125. Miller, *Mr. Crump of Memphis*, 130.
126. *Commercial Appeal*, September 2, 1924, 11.
127. Michie and Ryhlick, *Dixie Demagogues*, 245.
128. *Commercial Appeal*, September 2, 1924, 11.
129. Ibid.
130. Perry, *Democracy Begins at Home*, 33.
131. Michie and Ryhlick, *Dixie Demagogues*, 252.
132. Perry, *Democracy Begins at Home*, 36, 37.
133. *Commercial Appeal*, January 16, 1924, 6.
134. Miller, *Mr. Crump of Memphis*, 130; interview with Chandler, November 12, 1965.
135. Phillips, "Rowlett Paine, Mayor of Memphis," 107.
136. Interview with Chandler.
137. Allen, *Only Yesterday*, 46, 47; Chalmers, *Hooded Americanism*, 152.
138. Phillips, "Rowlett Paine, Mayor of Memphis," 112; interview with Hinds; Miller, *Mr. Crump of Memphis*, 138; interview with Chandler.

Chapter 6

139. *Commercial Appeal*, January 2, 1924, 14.
140. Ibid.
141. Ibid., March 29, 1924, 6.
142. Ibid., January 6, 1924, 16.
143. Ibid., January 4, 1924, 11.
144. Ibid., January 3, 1924, 8.
145. Ibid.
146. Ibid., January 8, 1924, 1.
147. *News Scimitar* (Memphis), January 15, 1924, 1.
148. *Commercial Appeal*, January 16, 1924, 6.
149. Interview with Bejach.
150. *Commercial Appeal*, January 22, 1924, 11.
151. *News Scimitar*, January 29, 1924, 1; *Commercial Appeal*, February 26, 1924, 10.
152. *Commercial Appeal*, January 17, 1924, 11.
153. Ibid., February 16, 1924, 11; February 26, 1924, 5.
154. Ginger, *Six Days or Forever?*, 182.

Chapter 7

155. *Commercial Appeal*, February 29, 1924, 13.
156. *Papers of Kenneth D. McKellar*, K.D. McKellar to Martha McKellar, March 5, 1924.
157. Ibid., John D. Martin to K.D. McKellar, April 2, 1924.
158. Ibid., K.D. McKellar to J.A. Riechman, March 5, 1924.
159. Ibid., E.H. Crump to K.D. McKellar, April 21, 1924.
160. Ibid., K.D. McKellar to R.L. McKellar, May 29, 1924.
161. *Commercial Appeal*, May 31, 1924, 11.
162. Ibid., June 27, 1924, 10.
163. Ibid., June 30, 1924, 9.
164. Allen, *Only Yesterday*, 136; Sann, *Lawless Decade*, 202.
165. *Commercial Appeal*, July 13, 1924, 13.
166. Ibid., June 1, 1924, 14; June 10, 1924, 19.
167. Ibid., June 22, 1924, 12.
168. Ibid., July 6, 1924, 14.
169. *News Scimitar*, July 8, 1924, 1.
170. *Commercial Appeal*, July 8, 1924, 13.

171. Ibid., July 30, 1924, 24.

172. Ibid., August 2, 1924, 8.

173. Ibid., August 5, 1924, 6.

174. Interview with Marks.

175. *Commercial Appeal*, June 27, 1916, 6.

176. *Papers of Kenneth D. McKellar*, K.D. McKellar to E.B. Stahlman, August 21, 1924; *News Scimitar*, August 7, 1924, 6.

177. Miller, *Mr. Crump of Memphis*, 357.

178. *Commercial Appeal*, August 6, 1924, 1.

179. *News Scimitar*, August 8, 1924, 1; *Commercial Appeal*, August 8, 1924, 1.

180. *News Scimitar*, August 8, 1924, 1; *Commercial Appeal*, August 8, 1924, 1.

181. *News Scimitar*, November 9, 1923, 1; August 8, 1924, 1; *Fourteenth Census of the United States Taken in the Year 1920*, vol. 3, *Population*, Department of Commerce (Washington, D.C.: U.S. Government Printing Office, 1922), 977–99; interview with Hinds.

182. *News Scimitar*, August 8, 1924, 1.

183. Ibid.

184. Michie and Ryhlick, *Dixie Demagogues*, 247.

185. *Commercial Appeal*, August 9, 1924, 1.

186. *News Scimitar*, August 28, 1924, 10.

187. Ibid., September 10, 1924, 19.

188. Ibid., February 26, 1925, 13.

189. Ibid., March 17, 1925, 1.

190. Interview with Bejach.

191. *Papers of Kenneth D. McKellar*, E.H. Crump to K.D. McKellar, August 1, 1925.

192. *Commercial Appeal*, October 31, 1924, 11.

193. Ibid., October 26, 1924, 8.

194. *Papers of Kenneth D. McKellar*, K.D. McKellar to Austin Peay, September 3, 1924.

195. *Commercial Appeal*, November 5, 1924, 1.

Chapter 8

196. Allen, *Only Yesterday*, 61 *et seq.*

197. *Commercial Appeal*, January 25, 1925, 10.

198. Ibid., February 16, 1926, 13.

199. Ibid., January 8, 1926, 13.

200. Ibid., September 10, 1925, 16.
201. Ibid., September 16, 1925, 1,6.
202. Ibid., January 25, 1926, 3.
203. Ibid., January 23, 1924, 6.
204. Ibid., February 27, 1924, 6.
205. Ibid., February 22, 1925, 3,7.
206. Ibid., March 9, 1924, 10.
207. Couch, *Culture in the South*, 187.
208. *Commercial Appeal*, January 16, 1924, 7.
209. Cash, *Mind of the South*, 385.
210. *Commercial Appeal*, January 16, 1924, 7.
211. Ibid., January 24, 1924, 6; Talbot, *Entertainer*, 116.
212. *Commercial Appeal*, January 16, 1924, 7.
213. Hall, *Best Remaining Seats*, 24.
214. *Commercial Appeal*, January 4, 1924,1.
215. Ibid., January 24, 1924, 6.

Chapter 9

216. McIlwaine, *Memphis Down in Dixie*, 22.
217. *Commercial Appeal*, May 18, 1924, 16; May 25, 1925, 1.
218. *Papers of Kenneth D. McKellar*, Rowlett Paine to K.D. McKellar, December 3, 1923.
219. *Commercial Appeal*, May 25, 1925, 1.
220. *Press-Scimitar*, October 28, 1980, 9B.
221. *Commercial Appeal*, January 1, 1924, 1.
222. Ibid., March 11, 1924, 6.
223. Ibid., January 1, 1924, 6; January 5, 1924, 6, 10.
224. Ibid., January 1, 1926, 6, 12.
225. Ibid., May 18, 1924, 16.
226. Ibid., April 23, 1927, 6.
227. Ibid., August 2, 1924, 6.
228. Ibid., February 24, 1926, 7.
229. Ibid., January 1, 1926, 12.
230. Ibid., June 2, 1927, 11.

Chapter 10

231. Ginger, *Six Days or Forever?*, 14.
232. *Commercial Appeal*, February 8, 1924, 11.
233. Ibid., July 17, 1924, 1.
234. Cash, *Mind of the South*, 296.
235. *Commercial Appeal*, April 6, 1924, 1; *Time*, October 10, 1955.
236. *Commercial Appeal*, April 7, 1924, 1–2.
237. Ibid., April 10, 1924, 1; April 7, 1924, 1; April 13, 1924, 1.
238. Ibid., May 14, 1924, 1; May 19, 1924, 1; May 15, 1924, 1.
239. Ibid., February 10, 1925, 12.
240. Ibid., May 21, 1924, 1; May 22, 1924, 1.
241. Ibid., May 31, 1924, 12.
242. Ibid., May 29, 1924, 5.
243. Ibid., January 26, 1925, 1, 11.
244. Ginger, *Six Days or Forever?*, 10–12.
245. Ibid., 83.
246. *Commercial Appeal*, August 23, 1925, 1.
247. Ibid., July 12, 1925, 6.
248. *Papers of Kenneth D. McKellar*, E.H. Crump to Hill McAlister, August 14, 1925.
249. Ibid.
250. Ibid.
251. *Commercial Appeal*, June 28, 1925, section IV, 8.
252. Ibid., June 25, 1925, 11.
253. Ibid.; July 4, 1925, 8; Ginger, *Six Days or Forever?*, 73.
254. *Commercial Appeal*, July 4, 1925, 8.
255. Ibid., July 22, 1925, 1.
256. Couch, *Culture in the South*, 150.
257. *Papers of Kenneth D. McKellar*, E.H. Crump to K.D. McKellar, January 5, 1926.

Chapter 11

258. Miller, *Memphis during the Progressive Era*, 125.
259. Miller, *Mr. Crump of Memphis*, 108; *State ex rel. v. Riechman*, 135 Tenn. 657, *et seq.* (1916).
260. Interview with Hinds.

261. *Commercial Appeal*, February 6, 1924, 11; February 7, 1924, 15; August 22, 1924, 1; February 16, 1924, 6; interview with Hinds; O'Daniel, *Crusaders, Gangsters and Whiskey*, 151.

262. *Commercial Appeal*, May 25, 1925, 1.

263. Ibid., February 7, 1926, 6; Simkins, *South Old and New*, 264.

264. Interview with Hinds.

265. *New York Times*, September 23, 1927, 29.

266. *Commercial Appeal*, October 6, 1927, 1.

267. Ibid., June 28, 1927, 1.

268. Lee, *Beale Street*, 101.

269. *Commercial Appeal*, June 28, 1927, 1.

270. Ibid., July 2, 1927, 13.

271. Ibid., July 3, 1927, 1.

272. Ibid., July 11, 1927, 1; July 18, 1927, 13; July 13, 1927, 1.

273. Ibid., August 16, 1927, 1; August 17, 1927, 1; October 23, 1927, 1.

274. Ibid., September 23, 1927, 1; September 25, 1927, 1.

275. Ibid., October 6, 1927, 1.

276. Ibid., October 7, 1927, 6.

277. Ibid., October 22, 1927, 13.

278. Ibid., October 13, 1927, 1.

279. Ibid.

280. Ibid., October 18, 1927, 13.

281. Lee, *Beale Street*, 101.

282. *Commercial Appeal*, March 11, 1928, 1.

Chapter 12

283. McIlwaine, *Memphis Down in Dixie*, 269; *Press Scimitar*, August 13, 1964, 11; Brooks, "Annals of Finance,"130, 131.

284. *Commercial Appeal*, February 24, 1924, 1.

285. Ibid., March 6, 1924, 2.

286. Ibid., March 8, 1924, 1.

287. Ibid., March 7, 1924, 1.

288. Ibid., March 9, 1924, 10.

289. Ibid., March 31, 1924, 1.

290. Ibid., March 30, 1924, 1; January 23, 1926, 9.

291. McIlwaine, *Memphis Down in Dixie*, 271.

292. *Commercial Appeal*, April 2, 1925, 12.

293. Ibid., April 5, 1925, 13, 14.

294. Ibid., November 6, 1925, 15.

295. Ibid.

296. Ibid., October 4, 1925, 15. "Restricted" probably meant no Jews allowed.

297. McIlwaine, *Memphis Down in Dixie*, 277.

298. Ibid., 272.

299. *Press Scimitar*, August 13, 1964, 11.

Chapter 13

300. May, *End of American Innocence*, 82; Cash, *Mind of the South*, 272.

301. *Commercial Appeal*, January 4, 1916, 7; *News Scimitar*, January 8, 1916, 2.

302. Carey, "Changing Image of the South," 3.

303. *Commercial Appeal*, February 12, 1925, 11.

304. Asbury, *French Quarter*, 106–13.

305. *Commercial Appeal*, January 29, 1924, 1; January 3, 1926, 1.

306. Ibid., June 4, 1924, 6, 9, 13.

307. Ibid., June 3, 1924, 13.

308. Ibid., June 7, 1924, 1.

309. Ibid., June 3, 1924, 13.

310. Ibid., June 4, 1924, 2.

311. Ibid., June 7, 1924, 11.

312. Ibid., June 7, 1924, 1.

Chapter 14

313. Capers, *Biography of a River Town*, 164; U.S. Census of 1920, 977.

314. Miller, *Memphis during the Progressive Era*, 6.

315. Ibid., 132.

316. U.S. Census of 1920, 977; *News Scimitar*, August 8, 1924, 1; *Commercial Appeal*, August 2, 1924, 1.

317. Taylor, Peay and Paine were opposed by Crump in the elections discussed.

318. U.S. Census of 1920, 977, 978, 979; *News Scimitar*, August 6, 1926, 1; *Press-Scimitar*, November 11, 1927, 17.

319. *Press-Scimitar*, November 11, 1927, 17.

320. Perry, *Democracy Begins at Home*, 36, 37.

321. Lee, *Beale Street*, 247.

322. *Commercial Appeal*, February 28, 1924, 24.

323. Cash, *Mind of the South*, 307.

324. *Commercial Appeal*, July 5, 1924, 18.

325. Ibid., January 1, 1925, 1; January 2, 1925, 6.

326. Cash, *Mind of the South*, 308, 315.

327. Ibid., 310.

328. *Commercial Appeal*, August 13, 1927, 1.

329. Ibid., September 21, 1925, 1.

330. Ibid., April 22, 1927, 10.

331. Ibid., September 22, 1925, 3.

332. Ibid., September 29, 1927, 13.

333. Ibid., January 12, 1924, 6.

334. Ibid., January 9, 1926, 13.

335. Ibid., January 1, 1919, 5.

336. May, *End of American Innocence*, 82; Grantham, *Democratic South*, 67.

337. Lee, *Beale Street*, 205.

338. *Commercial Appeal*, June 18, 1925, 5.

339. Ginger, *Six Days or Forever?*, 19, 20.

340. *Papers of Kenneth D. McKellar*, E.H. Crump to K.D. McKellar, April 24, 1928; Miller, *Mr. Crump of Memphis*, 29.

341. *Commercial Appeal*, August 10, 1924, 2.

342. Ibid., September 13, 1925, 13.

343. Ibid., July 31, 1924, 11.

344. Ibid., March 16, 1924, 6.

345. Interview with Marks.

346. *Commercial Appeal*, August 26, 1925, 13.

347. Ibid., March 19, 1924, 1.

348. Ibid., October 2, 1925, 18.

349. Ibid., March 22, 1924, 13.

350. Ibid., October 8, 1925, 6.

351. Ibid., May 9, 1925, 1; April 15, 1965, 6.

352. Ibid., July 22, 1925, 1; October 4, 1925, 1; August 18, 1972, sec. 6: 7, 8.

353. Ibid., February 14, 1925, 1.

354. Hutchins, *What Happened in Memphis*, 104.

355. Lee, *Beale Street*, 259.

356. Ibid., 253.

357. McIlwaine, *Memphis Down in Dixie*, 321–22; interview with Chandler.

358. Interview with Chandler.

359. Hutchins, *What Happened in Memphis*, 104.

360. *Commercial Appeal*, January 3, 1924, 5.

361. Ibid., April 13, 1924, 23.

362. Ibid., May 2, 1924, 13; Lee, *Beale Street*, 264.

363. Lee, *Beale Street*, 265.

364. *News Scimitar*, August 3, 1924, 9.

365. Ibid., October 7, 1924, 13; Lee, *Beale Street*, 266.

366. *News Scimitar*, July 10, 1925, 1.

367. *Papers of Kenneth D. McKellar*, William D. Kyser to K.D. McKellar, July 10, 1925.

368. *Commercial Appeal*, July 24, 1925, 9.

369. Ibid., September 19, 1925, 1; Lee, *Beale Street*, 267.

370. *Papers of Kenneth D. McKellar*, William Metcalf to K.D. McKellar, December 17, 1925.

371. Ibid., S.E. Murray to K.D. McKellar, January 8, 1926.

372. Lee, *Beale Street*, 268.

373. *Papers of Kenneth D. McKellar*, K.D. McKellar to C.P.J. Mooney, January 25, 1926.

374. Ibid., E.H. Crump to K.D. McKellar, January 19, 1926.

375. Ibid., K.D. McKellar to Harry B. Anderson, January 29, 1926.

376. Ibid., E.H. Crump to K.D. McKellar, February 2, 1926.

377. Ibid., K.D. McKellar to H.C. McKellar, April 12, 1926.

378. Lee, *Beale Street*, 267.

379. *Papers of Kenneth D. McKellar*, H.C. McKellar to K.D. McKellar, April 10, 1926.

380. *Commercial Appeal*, June 23, 1927, 13.

Chapter 15

381. Ibid., October 3, 1925, 17.

382. Ibid., March 5, 1925, 10.

383. Ibid., July 2, 1925, 13.

384. Ibid., July 3, 1925, 11.

385. *Papers of Kenneth D. McKellar*, E.H. Crump to K.D. McKellar, July 14, 1925.

386. *Commercial Appeal*, March 19, 1925, 6.

387. Interview with Chandler.

388. *Commercial Appeal*, August 28, 1925, 13.

389. Ibid., October 1, 1925, 19; October 2, 1925, 18.

390. Ibid., October 24, 1925, 13.

391. Ibid., April 29, 1927, 14.

392. Ibid., January 22, 1924, 11.

393. Ibid., March 21, 1925, 13.

394. McFerrin, *Caldwell and Company*, 102.

395. Miller, *Mr. Crump of Memphis*, 70.

396. McFerrin, *Caldwell and Company*, 100.

397. Interview with Bejach.

398. Folmsbee, Corlew and Mitchell, *History of Tennessee*, 348.

399. *Papers of Kenneth D. McKellar*, E.H. Crump to K.D. McKellar, August 14, 1925.

400. Folmsbee, Corlew and Mitchell, *History of Tennessee*, 348.

401. *Papers of Kenneth D. McKellar*, E.H. Crump to K.D. McKellar, February 15, 1926.

402. Ibid., E.H. Crump to K.D. McKellar, April 1, 1926.

403. *Commercial Appeal*, July 18, 1926, 1.

404. Ibid.

405. Ibid., August 5, 1926, 1.

406. Ibid., August 4, 1926, 1.

407. *News Scimitar*, August 2, 1926, 1.

408. Folmsbee, Corlew and Mitchell, *History of Tennessee*, 349.

409. *Commercial Appeal*, August 6, 1926, 1. Apparently, there was no literacy test in Tennessee.

410. *Commercial Appeal*, August 6, 1926, 6.

411. Ibid., August 6, 1926, 10.

412. *News Scimitar*, August 7, 1926, 1.

413. Ibid., August 6, 1926, 1.

414. Ibid., August 6 and 8, 1924, 1. The vote in the First Precinct of the Tenth Ward, mentioned by the *Commercial Appeal*, was double that of the 1924 election; but the vote in Ward 10, Precinct 2 was smaller. There was a decrease in the Twelfth Ward compared to 1924.

415. *News Scimitar*, August 7, 1926, 1.

416. Ibid., August 6, 1926, 1.

417. Bridges, "Editor Mooney vs. Boss Crump," 129.

418. *Papers of Kenneth D. McKellar*, K.D. McKellar to E.B. Stahlman, August 14, 1926.

419. Ibid., E.H. Crump to K.D. McKellar, April 8, 1926.

420. *News Scimitar*, August 7, 1926, 1.

421. *Papers of Kenneth D. McKellar*, Watkins Overton to K.D. McKellar, November 4, 1926.

422. Ibid., E.H. Crump to K.D. McKellar, April 8, 1926.

423. Folmsbee, Corlew and Mitchell, *History of Tennessee*, 349.

424. Miller, *Mr. Crump of Memphis*, 141.

425. *Papers of Kenneth D. McKellar*, Watkins Overton to K.D. McKellar, January 8, 1926.

426. Ibid., Watkins Overton to K.D. McKellar, January 3, 1927.

427. Ibid., Watkins Overton to K.D. McKellar, January 20 and February 4, 1927.

428. Ibid., Watkins Overton to K.D. McKellar, January 20, 1927.

429. Ibid., Watkins Overton to K.D. McKellar, February 4, 1927.

430. Ibid., Watkins Overton to K.D. McKellar, January 8, 1927.

Chapter 16

431. Gedye, "River and River Engineering," 328–29.

432. *Commercial Appeal*, April 15, 1927, 9.

433. Ibid., April 15, 1927, 15.

434. Interview with Marks.

435. *Commercial Appeal*, April 15, 1927, 15.

436. Ibid., April 24, 1927, 1.

437. Ibid., April 19, 1927, 11.

438. Ibid., April 21, 1927, 1.

439. Ibid., April 22, 1927, 1.

440. Ibid., May 3, 1927, 1, 8.

441. Ibid., April 27, 1927, 10; April 29, 1927, 13.

442. Hays, "Tennessee's Ed Crump," 51.

443. Walter White, "The Negro and the Flood," *Nation* (June 22, 1927), 688–89, quoted in Carey, "Changing Image of the South," 18.

444. *Commercial Appeal*, April 24, 1927, 1.

445. Ibid., May 1, 1927, 1.

446. Ibid., July 31, 1927, 17.

447. Ibid., August 3, 1927, 1.

448. Ibid., April 27, 1927, 6.

Chapter 17

449. *Louisville Courier Journal*, September 14, 1924, 6.

450. Bartholomew, *Comprehensive City Plan*.

451. *Commercial Appeal*, December 30, 1924, 12.

452. Ibid., July 27, 1924, 10.

453. Ibid., March 1, 1924, 11; *News Scimitar*, June 19, 1925, 1.

454. *Commercial Appeal*, December 3, 1925, 16.

455. Ibid., January 19, 1925, 8.

456. Interview with Bejach.

457. *Commercial Appeal*, June 1, 1927, 1.

458. Ibid., June 21, 1927, 11; June 23, 1927, 11.

459. Ibid., July 27, 1927, 1.

460. Ibid., July 28, 1927, 1.

461. Ibid., July 2, 1927, 13.

462. Ibid., July 3, 1927, 6.

463. Ibid.

464. Ibid., July 24, 1927, 13.

465. Ibid., July 31, 1927, 1.

466. Miller, *Mr. Crump of Memphis*, 141, 142.

467. *Commercial Appeal*, August 21, 1927, 1.

468. Ibid., August 24, 1927, 13.

469. Ibid., August 31, 1927, 1.

470. Interview with Chandler.

471. *Commercial Appeal*, September 1, 1927, 1.

472. Ibid., September 9, 1927, 1.

473. Ibid., September 15, 1927, 1.

474. Ibid., September 18, 1927, 1.

475. Ibid., September 27, 1927, 1.

476. Ibid., September 21, 1927, 1.

477. Interview with Bejach.

478. *Commercial Appeal*, October 5, 1927, 13.

479. Ibid., October 8, 1927, 11.

480. Ibid., October 9, 1927, 16.

481. Ibid., October 14, 1927, 15.

482. Ibid., October 13, 1927, 13.

483. Ibid., October 20, 1927, 15.

484. Ibid., October 23, 1927, 1.

485. Ibid., October 25, 1927, 1.

486. Ibid., October 26, 1927, 1.

487. Ibid., October 28, 1927, 1.

488. Ibid., October 29, 1927, 13.

489. Ibid., October 30, 1927, 21.

490. Lee, *Beale Street*, 244–47.

491. Interview with Chandler.

492. *Commercial Appeal*, September 9, 1927, 13.

493. Ibid.

494. Ibid., September 10, 1927, 11.

495. Ibid.

496. Ibid., September 11, 1927, 1.

497. Ibid., November 1, 1927, 11.

498. Ibid., November 2, 1927, 11.

499. Interview with Brenner.

500. *Commercial Appeal*, November 7, 1927, 1.

501. Interview with Bejach.

502. *Commercial Appeal*, November 8, 1927, 1.

503. Ibid., November 8, 1927, 13.

504. Ibid.

505. Interview with Marks.

506. *Commercial Appeal*, November 9, 1927, 6.

507. Ibid., November 9, 1927, 6. Mooney died in November 1926. Although no friend of Crump's, it has been suggested that new owner Nashvillian Luke Lea wanted to avoid anything that would stir Crump against his future political ambitions. Baker, *Memphis Commercial Appeal*, 278–79.

508. *Commercial Appeal*, November 10, 1927, 1.

509. Ibid., October 18, 1927, 1; October 19, 1927, 1.

510. Ibid., October 23, 1927, 1.

511. Ibid., November 11, 1927, 4.

512. Interview with Bejach.

513. *Commercial Appeal*, November 11, 1927, 1.

514. Ibid.

515. Ibid.

516. Ibid.

Chapter 18

517. Ibid., November 11, 1927, 6.

518. Perry, *Democracy Begins at Home*, 33.
519. *Papers of Kenneth D. McKellar*, E.H. Crump to K.D. McKellar, December 16, 1927.
520. *Commercial Appeal*, May 26, 1928, 1.

BIBLIOGRAPHY

Printed Works

Abels, Jules. *In the Time of Silent Cal.* New York: G.P. Putnam's Sons, 1969.

Allen, Frederick Lewis. *Only Yesterday.* New York: Harper and Brothers, 1931.

Asbury, Herbert. *The French Quarter.* New York: Garden City Publishing Co., Inc., 1938.

Baker, Thomas Harrison. *The Memphis Commercial Appeal.* Baton Rouge: Louisiana State University Press, 1971.

Bartholomew, Harland. *A Comprehensive City Plan, Memphis, Tennessee.* Memphis, TN: City Planning Commission, 1924.

Beard, Charles E., and Mary R. Beard. *America in Midpassage.* New York: Macmillan Co., 1939.

Book of Three States: The Notable Men of Mississippi, Arkansas and Tennessee. Memphis, TN: Commercial Appeal Publishing Company, 1914.

Capers, Gerald M. *The Biography of a River Town.* New Orleans: Gerald M. Capers, 1966.

Cash, W.J. *The Mind of the South.* New York: Alfred A. Knopf, Inc., 1941.

Chalmers, David M. *Hooded Americanism.* Garden City, NY: Doubleday & Co., 1965.

Church, Annette E., and Roberta Church. *The Robert R. Churches of Memphis.* Ann Arbor, MI: Edwards Bros., 1974.

Coppock, Paul R. *Memphis Sketches.* Memphis, TN: Friends of Memphis and Shelby County Libraries, 1976.

Couch, W.T., ed. *Culture in the South*. Chapel Hill: University of North Carolina Press, 1935.

De Camp, L. Sprague. *The Great Monkey Trial*. Garden City, NY: Doubleday & Co., 1968.

Folmsbee, Stanley J., Robert E. Corlew and Enoch L. Mitchell. *History of Tennessee*. Vol. 2. New York: Lewis Historical Publishing Co., Inc., 1960.

Ginger, Ray. *Six Days or Forever?* New York: Signet Books, 1960.

Grantham, Dewey W. *The Democratic South*. New York: W.W. Norton & Co., Inc., 1963.

Hall, Ben M. *The Best Remaining Seats*. New York: Bramhall House, 1961.

Handy, W.C. *Father of the Blues*. New York: Macmillan Co., 1941.

House, Boyce. *Cub Reporter*. New York: Hightower Press, 1947.

Hutchins, Fred L. *What Happened in Memphis*. Memphis, TN: privately printed, 1965.

Kelley, Camille. *A Friend in Court*. New York: Dodd, Mead & Co., 1942.

Lee, George Washington. *Beale Street: Where the Blues Began*. New York: R.O. Ballou, 1934.

Lynd, Robert S., and Helen Merrell Lynd. *Middletown: A Study in American Culture*. New York: Harcourt Brace & World, Inc., 1929.

Martin, Ralph G. *The Bosses*. New York: G.P. Putnam's Sons, 1964.

May, Henry F. *The End of American Innocence*. New York: Alfred Knopf, 1959.

Maynard, John. *The Roaring Twenties*. New York: Literary Enterprises, Inc., 1955.

McFerrin, John Berry. *Caldwell and Company: A Southern Financial Empire*. Chapel Hill: University of North Carolina Press, 1939.

McIlwaine, Shields. *Memphis Down in Dixie*. New York: E.P. Dutton & Co., Inc., 1948.

Mencken, H.L. *The Vintage Mencken*. Alastair Cooke, ed. New York: Vintage Books, 1961.

Mercer, Charles, *Legion of Strangers*. New York: Holt, Reinhart and Winston, 1964.

Michie, Alan Andres, and Frank Ryhlick. *Dixie Demagogues*. New York: Vanguard Press, 1939.

Miller, William D. *Memphis During the Progressive Era, 1900–1917*. Memphis, TN: Memphis State University Press, 1957.

———. *Mr. Crump of Memphis*. Baton Rouge: Louisiana State University Press, 1964.

Mitchell, Broadus, and George Sinclair. *The Industrial Revolution in the South*. Baltimore, MD: Johns Hopkins Press, 1930.

Mooney, C.P.J. *The Mid-South and Its Builders*. Memphis, TN: Mid-South Biographic and Historical Association, 1920.

Mowry, George E. *The Urban Nation, 1920–1960*. New York: Hill and Wang, 1965.

O'Daniel, Patrick. *Crusaders, Gangsters and Whiskey*. Jackson: University of Mississippi Press, 2018.

Perry, Jennings. *Democracy Begins at Home: The Tennessee Fight on the Poll Tax*. Philadelphia: J.P. Lippincott Company, 1944.

Sann, Paul. *The Lawless Decade*. New York: Crown Publishers, Inc., 1957.

Simkins, Francis Butler. *The South Old and New: A History, 1820–1947*. New York: Alfred A. Knopf, 1947.

Steinberg, Alfred. *The Bosses*. New York: Macmillan Co., 1972.

Talbot, Margaret. *The Entertainer*. New York: Riverhead Books, 2012.

Tucker, David M. *Lieutenant Lee of Beale Street*. Nashville, TN: Vanderbilt University Press, 1971.

U.S. House of Representatives. *Hearing Before the Special Committee Regarding Conduct of Harry B. Anderson, United States District Judge, Western District of Tennessee, November 18–20, 1930*. Washington, D.C.: U.S. Government Printing Office, 1931.

Vance, Rupert B. *Human Factors in Cotton Culture*. Chapel Hill: University of North Carolina Press, 1929.

White, William Allen. *A Puritan in Babylon*. New York: Macmillan Company, 1938.

Williams, T. Harry. *Romance and Realism in Southern Politics*. Athens: University of Georgia Press, 1961.

Young, J.P. *Standard History of Memphis, Tennessee*. Knoxville, TN: H.W. Crew and Co., 1912.

Unpublished Material

Bridges, Lamar Whitlow. "Editor Mooney vs. Boss Crump." Unpublished master's thesis, University of Wisconsin (Journalism), 1963.

Carey, Patrick. "The Changing Image of the South in the 1920s." Unpublished senior thesis, San Francisco State College, 1965.

Connell, Mary Ann Strong. "The Peabody Hotel." Unpublished master's thesis, University of Mississippi (History), 1971.

Geraghty, Sister Mary Leontina. "The Life and Editorials of C.P.J. Mooney." Unpublished master's thesis, Creighton University (English), 1932.

Hays, Andrew J. "Tennessee's Ed Crump: A Study of His Life and Career." Unpublished senior thesis, Harvard University, 1960.

McKellar, Kenneth D. Correspondence and collected papers. Memphis Public Library, Memphis, Tennessee.

Phillips, Virginia M. "Rowlett Paine's First Term as Mayor of Memphis, 1920–1924." Unpublished master's thesis, Memphis State University (History), 1958.

Stanton, Imelda, ed. "Blocked Commercial Appeal Editorials by C.P.J. Mooney." Unpublished manuscript, vols. 5, 6 and 7 for 1923.

Periodicals

American Heritage 16, no. 5 (August 1965).

Blankenship, Jerry R. "The *Commercial Appeal*'s Attack on the Ku Klux Klan." *West Tennessee Historical Society Papers* 31 (1977): 44–58.

Bridges, Lamar Whitlow. "Editor Mooney vs. Boss Crump." *West Tennessee Historical Society Papers* 20 (1966): 77–107.

Brooks, John. "Annals of Finance: A Corner in Piggly-Wiggly." *New Yorker Magazine,* June 6, 1959, 129–50.

Commercial Appeal, 1924–28.

Kitchens, Allen H. "Ouster of Mayor Edward H. Crump." *West Tennessee Historical Society Papers* 19 (1965): 105–20.

Louisville Courier Journal, September 14, 1924.

News Scimitar (Memphis), 1919–28.

New York Times, May 31, June 14, 1926; September 23, 1927.

Phillips, Virginia M. "Rowlett Paine, Mayor of Memphis 1920–1924." *West Tennessee Historical Society Papers* 13 (1959): 95–116.

Silver, James W. "C.P.J. Mooney of *The Commercial Appeal*, Crusader for Diversification." Reprinted from *Agricultural History* 17 (April 1943): 81–89.

Tilly, Bette B. "Memphis and the Mississippi Valley Flood." *West Tennessee Historical Society Papers* 14 (1970): 41–56.

Tindall, George B. "Business Progressivism: Southern Politics in the Twenties." *South Atlantic Quarterly* (Winter 1963): 101.

Watson, Robert M., Jr. "The Memphis Sound, 1913–1925, as Played by the Egyptians, etc." *West Tennessee Historical Society Papers* 25 (1971): 78.

Reference Works

Gedye, Nicholas G. "River and River Engineering." In *Encyclopedia Britannica* vol. 19, 1957, 328.

Interviews

Bejach, Lois D., judge, Tennessee Court of Appeals (1954–68); county attorney (1924–33); chancellor (judge) (1933–54). Personal interview, December 6, 1965.

Brenner, Lester, U.S. commissioner (magistrate) (1925–33); Republican election commissioner (1930–64). Personal interview, December 14, 1965.

Chandler, Walter, state senator (1921–23); U.S. congressman (Ninth District, Memphis) (1935–40); mayor of Memphis (1940–46, 1955); campaign manager for Overton-Davis ticket (1927); E.H. Crump lieutenant (1921–54). Personal interview, November 12, 1965.

Hinds, M.A., former Memphis police officer, police chief and Shelby County sheriff. Personal interview, April 14, 1966.

Marks, Robert, reporter for the *Commercial Appeal*; reporter for the *News Scimitar* (1920s); executive secretary to Rowlett Paine (June 1927–January 1928). Personal interview, November 5, 1965.

INDEX

ABOUT THE AUTHOR

Robert A. Lanier is a native Memphian and a retired judge. He did graduate studies in history and has published numerous legal and historical articles and books, his proudest work being a history of the little-known pre–World War I creation of the kingdom of Albania, which postponed the world war for a year. Although he made his career among what he calls "the teeming multitudes of rogues, idlers and wastrels" in the legal profession, he was always a frustrated amateur historian. He served two terms on the Tennessee Historical Commission and co-founded Memphis Heritage, the local historical preservation organization. A lifelong animal lover, he is a past president of the Memphis Humane Society. An ardent Anglophile, he is also a co-founder of the Dickens-inspired Pickwick Club & Gastronomic Society and permanent corresponding carbuncle of the local Sherlock Holmes Giant Rats of Sumatra scion society. He is also a lifelong movie fan.